INSIGHTS ON
Bridge
MOMENTS IN BIDDING

BOOK
1

MIKE LAWRENCE

BARON BARCLAY
BRIDGE SUPPLY
Practice. Play. Teach.

PUBLISHED BY:

Baron Barclay Bridge Supplies
3600 Chamberlain Lane, Suite 206
Louisville, KY 40242
U.S. & Canada 1-800-274-2221
Worldwide 502-426-0410
Fax 502-426-2044
www.baronbarclay.com

ISBN: 978-1-944201-23-4

Cover design by Mary Maier
Text design and composition by John Reinhardt Book Design

Printed in the United States of America

Foreword

AFTER WRITING OVER 25 books on bridge that discuss certain aspects of play, defense, system, or general bidding, I've begun a series of books aimed at turning aspiring players into good players. Note I don't say expert players. That will be the next step.

Bridge isn't a game where you can immerse yourself for six months and become a good player. There's just too much to learn. You have to start somewhere and then move in the right direction.

Typically, when you start playing in a club, you feel lost. After you get your feet on the ground, you still recognize that you aren't moving very fast. Going forward requires that you get good guidance. Many players at your club will offer advice.

Much of that advice, unfortunately, isn't very good.

This series of books includes hundreds of mini-lessons, complete with insights and advice you can count on. The material is devoted to situations and problems you will see at the table but not in other books.

This book (#1 in a series) won't make you an expert.

But these books will start you on the path to being a good player and a good partner.

Enjoy the trip.

Mike Lawrence

West Deals   +   No One Vulnerable

WEST	EAST
♠ 9 4	♠ J 7 3
♥ K Q 7	♥ A 9 4
♦ K Q 3 2	♦ A 6 5
♣ A Q 7 6	♣ K 5 4 2

WEST	NORTH	EAST	SOUTH
?			

THIS HAND IS really a simple one. Either West opens with 1NT or he doesn't. The question for West is whether bidding 1NT with two small spades is good bridge. This is a recurring theme which you would like to be aware of in advance.

My opinion is that 1NT is a fine bid. You can choose to have a headache in the bidding or in the play.

If you open 1♣ or 1♦ and partner bids 1♠, your headache will come up in the bidding. You have too much to bid 1NT and you have too little to bid 2NT. Other bids leave you awkwardly placed as well.

You won't be happy if partner responds 1♥. What would your best rebid be now? Just another headache.

If you reach 3NT, your headache will come up in the play. If the defenders lead a spade you may go down on a hand where 5♣ was cold.

However. Take a second look at the two hands. 5♣ is not cold. If clubs are 4-1, 5♣ won't make. Against that, 3NT will make for sure if spades are 4-4 or if they do not lead spades. If South is the one with five spades, North won't know to lead them and you will take nine or ten or eleven notrump tricks in no time.

For me, a 1NT–3NT auction is fine. I much prefer making a bid that describes my hand perfectly (more or less) than to make a bid which leaves me sadly placed if partner makes a bid I am not ready for.

North Deals + No One Vulnerable

	WEST		EAST
♠	Q J 8 7 6 5 3	♠	4 2
♥	10 7 6 5	♥	K Q J 3
♦	2	♦	Q J 10 7
♣	Q	♣	A 9 4

WEST	NORTH	EAST	SOUTH
	3♦	Pass	Pass
?			

THIS IS A typical balancing problem. North opens 3♦ and East, with a nice hand, is right to pass. Double is dangerous with only two spades and the hand is too weak for 3NT.

Not so easy for West when 3♦ is passed around to him. He has an interesting problem. He expects East to have some points. They have to be somewhere. The odds are that East has some of them and South has the remainder.

What West would like to do is bid 3♠ and have that end the auction.

Unfortunately, if West bids 3♠, East will often have a good enough hand that he is entitled to bid. Since West is really weak, passing it out is best. If East-West can make 3♠, East will have a good hand and he will raise, and you will find that you can't make 4♠.

POSTMORTEM

It's hard to pass but that's probably West's best bid.

On the hand East has here, he would probably bid 3NT. He has two diamond stoppers and good cards on the side.

West isn't a passed hand. He could have a sound opening bid, in which case East should bid 3NT.

If East does bid 3NT, it will go down a lot. West would probably bid something. Likely he would bid 4♠. That will go down and it's possible that it will be doubled.

There's something else here that's important.

If West was the dealer and wasn't vulnerable, some would open 3♠. Some would pass because of the four-card heart suit.

If West was in third seat, opening 3♠ would be routine. In third seat, preempts have little in common with preempts in first or second seat.

A professional player playing with a client was taking forever to make a play. After a five minute pause, he still hadn't decided what to do and he went back into his pondering mode. After a few more minutes of nothing, his opponent asked, "Are you getting paid by the hour?"

South Deals + No One Vulnerable

WEST	EAST
♠ K 6	♠ Q 9 8 5 3
♥ J 4	♥ A Q 9 8
♦ A Q	♦ 9 6
♣ A Q J 10 9 7 6	♣ 8 2

WEST	NORTH	EAST	SOUTH
			3♦
?			

WEST HAS A good hand and is justifiably annoyed when South opens 3♦. West is going to bid something. It's just a matter of what he is going to bid.

West has two obvious choices and one choice that is awful.

Double is not a viable bid. Partner will all too often insist on one of the majors and West doesn't have support. His realistic choices are 3NT and 4♣.

Important guideline: When an opponent preempts and you are thinking of bidding four of a minor, you should give serious consideration to bidding 3NT instead.

This hand can't guarantee nine tricks at notrump. But it can't guarantee ten tricks at clubs either. Frankly, whichever choice you prefer will need some help from partner. Since you get a game bonus if you make 3NT and only a partscore bonus if you make 4♣, 3NT gets the nod.

Note by the way that if you bid 4♣, you may reach 5♣. Since 5♣ requires eleven tricks and 3NT requires nine tricks, it should be clear to bid 3NT.

East has a modest hand. Perhaps he should look for a major-suit contract. I suggest he does not. The reason is that a 3NT overcall is poorly defined. It can be bid with a balanced fifteen-count or a shapely twenty-count. Since East is reasonably content with notrump and looking for a major is uncertain, passing it out is a good idea.

QUICKIE

Many years ago I was lucky to get to play with Grant Baze. Most players know him for various of his rules including this one:

"Six-five, come alive." This meant that if you have 6-5 distribution, you should do a lot of bidding. Here's one of my special moments with Grant in which he was an opponent.

I found myself in 3♣ with this unusual club-suit combination.

♣ A Q 8 7 4

♣ A J 10 3 2

A first for me. During the play, I had reason to think that Grant, on my right, had the ♣K. I played the suit thusly. I led the jack from my hand toward the dummy. When West played low, I played the ace, Grant playing low. I led the queen from dummy on the next trick and Grant took his king. At least he tried to. When I produced the ace, Grant did a double take that I would love to have been able to capture in a picture.

Grant was too numb to call the director. I did it for him. His last words before we started the next hand were, "I was sure I had a club trick."

South Deals + East-West Vulnerable

	WEST		EAST
♠	Q J 10 7 3	♠	2
♥	J 10 8 7 4	♥	K 9 6 2
♦	A 8	♦	Q J 4 2
♣	5	♣	A 10 8 3

WEST	NORTH	EAST	SOUTH
			1NT*
2♥**	Pass	3♥	All pass

*15–17   **DONT ♥+♠

BIDDING AGAINST A strong notrump is not a good way to make a living. Opener has sixteen points on average and if his partner has a few points, you may get clipped if you get into the bidding.

Experience has taught a firm lesson.

Do not bid when you have balanced hands with scattered points.

Do bid when you have good suits and good shape. Points are less important than the number of tricks you can expect.

Is the West hand worth bidding with? And, if you agree that it is worth a bid, do you have a convention for this hand?

Here is a brief rundown on how you can show this hand.

Cappelletti/Hamilton:	Bid 2♦ to show the majors.
DONT:	Bid 2♥ to show the majors.
Landy:	Bid 2♣ to show the majors.

You will notice that these three conventions have a way to show the majors, the two most important suits.

With any luck, you will find a fit and can hope to make something. In the auction shown here, the 2♥ bid is the DONT convention showing the majors. Vulnerable, you need two five-card suits, so this hand is normal.

East, with a good fit and some decent side values, is barely worth a raise to 3♥. Even though you do not press for games after a strong 1NT opening bid, it's reasonable to try for a game when you have a good fit with useful high cards.

South passes and West has to decide whether to go on to game.

My instinct would be to pass because I am vulnerable and my partner might expect a little more. If I were not vulnerable I would bid 2♥ with less than this, and in that light this is enough to go on to 4♥.

It is one thing to get into the bidding with a shapely hand. Often it is wise. It is less wise to push on to game when you have a minimum. East, remember, knows you have the majors and he only invited. With what is surely a minimum five-five hand, I would pass.

As it turns out, the hands fit well and 4♥ has some chances. If West had a little more, say the ♥Q too, he might bid 4♥.

When bidding against a strong notrump you shouldn't bother bidding if you are balanced. You may wish to double the notrump bid for penalty, if your system allows it.

Even with a six-card suit you shouldn't bid unless the suit is good or you have nice distribution.

♠ Q 9
♥ K 9 6 5 4 3
♦ A Q
♣ J 8 3

This twelve-point hand isn't good enough to bid with over a strong notrump. The suit is broken and other than the ♦AQ, the hand has nothing but dubious values.

♠ 3
♥ K Q 10 8 7 6
♦ A 10 9 7
♣ 8 2

This nine-point hand is worth a bid. Bid 2♥ by whatever means your system calls for. Your good suit and shape rate to take two or three more tricks than the previous hand, which had twelve high-card points.

♠ Q J 8
♥ Q J 7 4
♦ Q 9 6 2
♣ A K

Pass. You have almost the same values as opener but you do not have an opening lead you really like. If this hand was slightly better, it would be OK to double if that was for penalty.

♠ Q J 8
♥ Q J 10 8
♦ K 10 8 3
♣ A K

This hand has one more point and it has a solid lead in the ♥Q. You can double with this one if your system includes penalty doubles. Note, though, that DONT and Cappelletti do not use a penalty double. In fact, giving up a penalty double of a strong 1NT bid isn't a big loss.

In summation, I urge you to adopt a convention against a strong 1NT opening bid.

South Deals + East-West Vulnerable

	WEST		EAST
♠	K 9 4	♠	Q 10 7 6 5 2
♥	K Q 6 3	♥	9 4
♦	A Q J 5	♦	10 9 4
♣	J 3	♣	8 4

WEST	NORTH	EAST	SOUTH
			1♣
Dbl	1♠	Pass	2♣
Pass	Pass	2♠	3♣
All pass			

THIS IS AN informed auction with both East and West doing something good. West made a takeout double that was a bit over average. East was ready to bid spades but North beat him to it. What should East do about this? East should pass. A double by East shows at least seven high-card points and four spades. It would be a penalty double. A 2♠ bid by East can be used to show a variety of hands, but whatever it means, it shows a better hand.

East has to pass. West doesn't have enough to bid again so he passes South's 2♣ rebid.

Now the fun starts. East has a weak but goodish hand for spades and now, on the second round, he comes back in with 2♠. Should West do something when South bids 3♣? The answer is a clear no.

East's 2♠ bid is natural. It can't be a strong bid. If East had anything good, he would have bid earlier. Therefore, East must have five or more spades and a very weak hand. West's hand isn't good enough to compete further opposite what East rates to have so he passes. A good sequence with each player in turn making a thoughtful bid.

West Deals + North-South Vulnerable

	WEST		EAST
♠	6	♠	K Q J 7 4 3
♥	A J 10 7 6 5 2	♥	K
♦	K 7 6	♦	Q 10
♣	J 9	♣	A K Q 6

WEST	NORTH	EAST	SOUTH
3♥	Pass	3♠	Pass
3NT	Pass	4♥	All pass

IS THIS WEST hand worth a 3♥ bid? What do you think?

I think preempting is a combination of sanity and personality. If you like to mix it up and mess with your opponents' minds, it should be automatic to preempt with hands like this one. It is true that you might lose nine tricks and be down six if your dummy is broke. But that's just the pundits speaking. I like lots of preempting and can tell you that I am viewed as conservative in this matter.

East bids 3♠, which requires a partnership agreement. The most important aspect of East's 3♠ bid is that it is forcing. West has to bid again. From East's perspective, 4♠ could be the right contract, and 3♠ will help find out.

Most players accept the idea that 3♠ is forcing. The reason for this is that you must have a way to explore. If 3♠ is not forcing, then you have to shut your eyes and make guesses when you would rather explore. Playing 3♠ as not forcing is very narrow and rather infrequent.

Given that it is forcing, how should West continue? West doesn't have spade support so he can't raise to 4♠. But he does have to bid.

West bids 3NT. It doesn't promise clubs and diamonds are well stopped but it does promise a smattering of values outside the heart suit and it denies spade support. West did, after all, open with a preempt, which shows most of the stuff in the long suit. West does not rate to have a lot of side values.

East, not finding a spade fit, retreats to 4♥, which West is pleased to pass.

East had some interesting choices over 3♥. He could bid 3♠, 4♥, or even 4♠. Or, if he felt like going quietly, he could pass 3♥.

His choice of 3♠ was fine since there is a good chance that four of a major is worthwhile. All that is necessary is to find out which major is best.

East knew that notrump wasn't likely to make, so he went back to 4♥.

POSTMORTEM

The important thing here is that 3♠ is known to be forcing. If East has something like:

♠ Q J 8 6 5 4 2
♥ –
♦ Q 3 2
♣ 9 8 4

he just passes 3♥. East knows the partnership is in trouble and hopes 3♥ will be passed out.

West Deals   +   North-South Vulnerable

WEST		EAST	
♠	10 9 3	♠	K J 8 5 4 2
♥	A Q 5	♥	10 3
♦	A K 10 5 4 3	♦	9
♣	8	♣	Q 5 3 2

WEST	NORTH	EAST	SOUTH
1♦	Pass	1♠	Pass
2♦	Pass	2♠	Pass
4♠	All pass		

WEST HAS A standard rebidding problem when East responds 1♠. Some players will raise with three-card support, which makes 2♠ a choice. However, with such good diamonds, no one will object strongly to rebidding 2♦.

East has enough spades to rebid 2♠. How many spades does East show?

The answer has to be six. Some players rebid five-card spade suits thinking that opener needs to know how many he has. This is a losing tendency. Opener often has a singleton spade and has no choice but to pass, leaving responder in a five-one fit. I've seen this happen over and over again and the results are almost always the same. Bad.

Knowing that East has six spades makes West's rebid easy. ♠1093 is fine support for a rebid suit and the rest of the hand is solid. Opener bids 4♠.

In a way, opener should evaluate his hand as if responder had shown a weak two-bid. Imagine that you had the West hand and your partner opened 2♠. It would be correct to bid game without bothering to ask questions.

West has all the key ingredients. There are nine trumps, plus West has aces, a king, a working queen and great shape.

POSTMORTEM

Going back to East's 2♠ bid: If East has five spades, he shouldn't rebid them, even with a singleton diamond. East knows that opener has a six-card suit, which means diamonds are OK. There's a lot to be said for stopping the bidding with misfits.

Having bid to 4♠, East now has to make it. Looking at the East-West hands you can see that East has a decent play for eleven tricks. However, there are snags. On a bad day, 4♠ might go down three tricks. Good bidding often requires a little good fortune in the play.

West Deals + Both Sides Vulnerable

WEST	EAST
♠ A K	♠ Q 10 7 6 2
♥ Q 10 8 6 4	♥ A J 3
♦ A J 10 7 5	♦ 3 2
♣ 2	♣ J 8 3

WEST	NORTH	EAST	SOUTH
1♥	Pass	2♥	Pass
4♥	All pass		

WEST OPENS 1♥ hoping he can find a fit. If there is a fit, his hand will be worth a lot more than it is now.

East has options. He has five decent spades but he also has heart support. East has to decide if it is right to bid 1♠ or to raise hearts. This is one of my pet themes and if you have been reading my articles for a long time, you will have seen this discussion before.

In my opinion, raising hearts is the proper bid. 100%. It shows your points and it shows your support. Your partner should be able to make a good decision now, something that he won't be able to do if you bid 1♠.

Here's a different look at this hand. Say that you responded with 1♠. The auction would continue this way:

WEST	NORTH	EAST	SOUTH
1♥	Pass	1♠	Pass
2♦	Pass	2♥	Pass
?			

You will notice in the bidding box that there is a question mark for West's last bid. He is thinking about what to do. I ask you this simple question. If he thinks for a long time and regretfully passes, how do you feel? This is the question posed to Spock in the fourth Star Trek movie, the one where they saved the whales.

How do you feel?
How do you feel?
How do you feel?

I know that if I had bid the East hand this way, I would feel terrible when my partner thought and then passed. I would know that the reason for his passing was that he feared I did not have real heart support.

As you can see from the hand diagram, your partner was indeed worried about his heart suit. If he knew you had good support, he wouldn't fret about the trumps. But thinking you might have given a preference with just two of them, he would do the right thing by passing it out in 2♥. Imagine this is the trump suit:

WEST	EAST
♥ Q 10 8 6 4	♥ 7 3

If East bids 1♠ and gives a preference to 2♥, opener is right to pass. If it turns out that East has good heart support and game turns out to be cold, it is responder's fault.

East Deals   +   North-South Vulnerable

	WEST		EAST
♠	8 7 6 3	♠	A K Q 5 4
♥	6 4 3 2	♥	5
♦	K J 5 4	♦	A 10 7 6
♣	3	♣	Q 7 2

WEST	NORTH	EAST	SOUTH
		1♠	Dbl
3♠	4♥	4♠	All pass

THIS IS ONE of my favorite themes. I travel all over the States teaching bridge. This auction inevitably comes up. When it does I take a vote and ask how many players play 1♠ - Dbl - 3♠ as preemptive. Even after years of this auction being discussed in print, about 25% of my group says they play the jump raise as limit.

Not a good treatment. Since you will have very few limit raises and since you will have a lot of hands like this one, it really is best to cater to the hands that come up and have a good bidding tactic available to use with them.

West has a pathetic little hand. When East bids 1♠ and South doubles, he has to decide if his hand is worth bidding with. It's fairly clear that if West bids 2♠, that won't buy the hand. By bidding 3♠ West tells East that he has some shape and he has four or more spades and he has from three to six high-card points. The three level should be safe and the bid might give East enough information that he can bid something.

Some players might feel that raising spades would just push the opponents into a cold game. How do you feel about that approach?

Today, players are bidding pretty accurately. It's not likely that a 3♠ bid would push them into a game they would not otherwise bid.

Note that the West hand has the ♦K. From his perspective that looks like a defensive trick. West has only a few teeth but he does have one nice defensive card.

As noted, raising to 3♠ here is fairly standard. Few bids have the pedigree that this one has. It goes back for many years.

Here is the rule that applies.

When your partner's opening bid is doubled, a jump raise by you is preemptive. It does not show a limit raise or a game-forcing raise, it shows a weak raise. You promise four trumps but only a few values. The hand that West has here is fine. It has the required four trumps and it has only four high-card points. It also has a little bit of shape.

East is able to compete to 4♠. On this hand it happens to be cold because the hands fit so well. The key is that East knows it's wise to bid 4♠, and the big piece of information that makes it possible is that East knows West has four spades.

If West had bid 2♠ or worse yet, if West passed over the double, East wouldn't know to bid 4♠.

POSTMORTEM

What should West bid if he has a true limit raise? For instance, what should West bid over South's double with these hands?

1.
    ♠ Q J 7 3
    ♥ A 4 3
    ♦ J 3
    ♣ Q 10 9 7

2.

♠ Q J 7 3
♥ A Q 3
♦ J 3
♣ Q J 7 2

There is a convention in use today called the Jordan 2NT bid. The way it works is worth knowing.

West bids 2NT with both of these hands. At the point West bids 2NT, he is announcing a limit raise in spades or a game-forcing raise in spades. In both cases he promises four-card support.

Opener will expect partner to have the limit raise. He usually bids 3♠ or 4♠.

If opener bids 3♠, responder passes when he has a limit raise (hand 1) and bids again when he has a game-forcing raise (hand 2).

The Jordan 2NT bid has been written up in many places including my book *Judgment at Bridge 2*. Page 152.

Do not use this convention when partner opens with a minor suit and the next player doubles. Doesn't work.

	HAND
	10

	WEST	EAST
♠	9	♠ Q J 8 3 2
♥	K 5 2	♥ A J 9 8
♦	A 5	♦ 8 7
♣	A K Q 10 6 5 3	♣ J 2

WEST	NORTH	EAST	SOUTH
1♣	2♦	Dbl	3♦
3NT	All pass		

WEST OPENS 1♣ and starts a small riot. North bids 2♦, weak, and East makes a negative double. South raises to 3♦. West would have liked a different auction but has to contend with this one.

What should West bid? It is not inconceivable that there is a slam. But finding out is almost impossible.

What West does bid is 3NT, a practical choice. West has eight likely tricks and needs only for one from East. It's possible to bid some number of clubs but since 5♣ would require eleven tricks, I rather like the 3NT bid. But I do not guarantee it.

On this hand 3NT is cold and 5♣ requires the heart finesse, something that's against the odds on the bidding.

Note that East didn't bid 4♠. West's 3NT bid was made under pressure and was something of a guess. East should feel content that he has some points which happen to include an ace. This is a good auction made under annoying circumstances.

West Deals　+　No One Vulnerable

	WEST		EAST
♠	9	♠	Q 7 4 3
♥	A K 10 6 3 2	♥	8
♦	K 8 6	♦	A 10
♣	K J 3	♣	A Q 10 9 5 2

WEST	NORTH	EAST	SOUTH
1♥	Pass	2♣	Pass
2♥	Pass	2♠	Pass
3♣	Pass	3NT	Pass
4♣	Pass	4♦	Pass
4NT	Pass	5♠	Pass
6♣	All pass		

THIS BIDDING USES the Two Over One system. There are a number of important issues in use here.

Firstly, East should respond 2♣, not 1♠. Here's the rule East follows:

RULE

When responder has game-going values, he always responds in his long suit. This means East should bid 2♣ first and then show the spades later. This sequence shows longer clubs than spades and allows opener to choose the best spot. If East bids spades first and then clubs, he shows that his spades are as long as or longer than the clubs. This misinformation can lead to trouble.

Opener repeats his hearts and East has to find a continuation. 2♠ is correct but some would bid 2NT or 3NT, which would be an error.

2♠ is not only best, it is mandatory. Opener could have four spades and you will miss your fit if you bid notrump. Notrump can always come later.

2♠ gets you a nice bid from opener. He goes back to 3♣. East has an easy 3NT bid.

Over 3NT, West continues with 4♣. West knows from East's two-over-one bid that East has an opening bid, most likely with five clubs. So far West has not shown a big hand and is just now catching up. Note that 4♣ is not Gerber. It is natural. Over 4♣ East cuebids 4♦ and the rest is relatively easy.

POSTMORTEM

East-West did well to reach 6♣. Now East has to make it. The defense leads a club, North following, so East won't be able to ruff two spades in dummy. He will have to set up the heart suit. Win the club in your hand and play the ♥A. Ruff a heart in your hand. With both opponents following to two rounds of hearts, the hand is over. Draw trumps, ending in dummy. If the hearts are 3-3, you have the rest. If hearts are 4-2, you can ruff a heart in your hand and will have to be content with twelve tricks.

This auction has a number of important points:

- East bids clubs and then spades.
- West does not insist on hearts. Six of a minor is a contract that is often overlooked. Here, the nice club fit was found early and West recognized that he had a good hand for clubs. Making 6♣ was a tie for top when the hand was played.

	WEST	EAST
♠	2	K 8 7 3
♥	A K 10 9 5 2	7 3
♦	K J 6	Q 8 3
♣	K Q 4	A 8 5 2

WEST	NORTH	EAST	SOUTH
1♥	Pass	1♠	Pass
3♥	Pass	?	

THIS IS AN easy problem to show. East is the one with the big decision. West opens 1♥ and jumps to 3♥ after East's 1♠ response.

Should East bid 3NT, 4♥, or pass?

It's easy to reject pass. West shows six hearts with about eighteen points so there is no misfit, and you have enough points to bid a game. The question is, which one?

In general, when you hear this auction, if your choice is to bid 3NT or to raise, you should raise when you have two-card support or more. Unless you have solid stoppers in the other suits, you may have a notrump weakness.

On this hand, you have stoppers in the other three suits but you can't be sure of nine tricks. I vote for 4♥. You know your side has eight hearts, which is a guideline that hearts will be a good trump suit.

POSTMORTEM

West has a typical hand. It turns out that 4♥ is more or less cold, going down only when terrible things happen to you. 3NT, however, is not safe. If the defenders lead spades, the suit you bid, they will set up enough tricks that 3NT is probably going down.

This is the kind of hand that can bid 3NT when holding two hearts:

♠ Q J 10 8
♥ 10 3
♦ K 10 9 6
♣ K Q 10

3NT should be OK since it rates to be safe from any attack. 4♥ is probably a safe bid but it could go down if the defenders can get a ruff or two.

QUICKIE

Partner opens 1♠. What is your best bid with this hand?

♠ K J 4
♥ 8 7 4
♦ A K J 3
♣ Q 8 7

Whatever you do, do not jump in spades and don't jump to 3NT. A jump raise of 1♥ or 1♠ promises four or more trumps. Further, do not jump to 2NT if you are using the Jacoby 2NT bid to show a game-forcing raise. You need four trumps here too. Bid 2♦ and then raise spades. When you don't raise spades right away, your partner will know you have three trumps. This is news your partner can use.

North Deals   +   No One Vulnerable

	WEST		EAST	
♠	4	♠	K Q J 9 7 3	
♥	K J 8 6	♥	3	
♦	A Q 9 3	♦	J 5 4	
♣	K J 10 2	♣	8 6 3	

WEST	NORTH	EAST	SOUTH
	Pass	2♠	Pass
?			

THIS HAND REQUIRES good judgment by both players. East opens a weak two-bid in spades. He has the necessary good suit and once you meet that requirement, you are usually right to make a weak two-bid.

The key for the rest of the auction is that West does not have enough points for game. East has a maximum of eleven (or ten if that is your agreement). West knows there is a misfit. This hand is not going to stretch to game. It is much better to pass. Not only do you stay in a contract that has a chance to make, you leave room for the opponents to make a mistake. If North doubles or bids a suit, you should get a nice penalty out of it.

My usual observation is that West must not sit there and futz around before passing 2♠. If he does that, North may realize that West has something and that may cause North to reject a possible balancing bid. And that is just what West is rooting for.

If West makes his pass in tempo, there's a fair chance that North will bid something. West has fourteen high-card points and East usually has between six and ten. This means that the opponents have up to twenty points. North is a passed hand but still, if he has ten or eleven of these points he may have something to think about. He will be hoping his partner has something, and you know North is going to be disappointed.

Remember this rule:

**DO NOT SHOW WHAT YOU HAVE
BY PASSING SLOWLY!**

Good players learn quickly to pass with misfits like this one. If you can you may catch some fish. You will not catch them if you sit and stew for a minute before passing.

East Deals + North-South Vulnerable

	WEST		EAST
♠	Q J 9 8 3	♠	10 7
♥	K J 10 6 5	♥	A Q 7
♦	J 5	♦	K Q 9 8
♣	8	♣	A 7 6 3

WEST	NORTH	EAST	SOUTH
		1NT	Pass
2♥	Pass	2♠	Pass
3♥	Pass	4♥	All pass

THIS HAND SHOWS a valuable bidding trick. East opens 1NT, catching West with an interesting hand. West has 5-5 in the majors and enough points that he is going to go to game. You may quibble that the West hand isn't worth forcing to game but the shape improves this hand a lot. The way to show 5-5 in the majors with game points is to respond 2♥, transferring to spades. East bids 2♠ and West bids 3♥. This is the agreement I am suggesting. West's 3♥ bid promises 5-5 and game points. West might have a huge hand. Here, East has support for hearts and a minimum notrump. So he raises to 4♥, and that's that.

The beauty of this understanding is that when West bids 3♥, he is showing 5-5. If West had a 5-4 hand he would start with Stayman.

This agreement by itself is good but it can be made better by adding some refinements.

Here's the beginning of the auction:

WEST	NORTH	EAST	SOUTH
		1NT	Pass
2♥	Pass	2♠	Pass
3♥	Pass	?	

The easy version of this is that East has some options with various hands he might have.

If East wants to play in spades:

He can bid 3♠. This bid says spades are trump.

He can bid 4♠. This bid says he has a nice hand for spades but he isn't interested in slam.

When East bids 3♠, West can raise to 4♠ or he can make a cuebid or he can ask for aces.

When East bids 4♠, West can ask for aces.

If East wants to play in hearts:

Here comes an important twist. If East likes hearts, he has options over West's 3♥ bid.

East can bid 4♥, which says he prefers hearts and has no interest in looking for a slam.

If East thinks there might be a slam, he can make a cuebid. This cuebid says hearts are trump. Not spades.

Remember that if East liked spades, he would have bid 3♠ or 4♠ over 3♥. All other bids show interest in hearts.

Some judgment is needed. But because responder has shown 5-5 in the majors and game points, the rest of the bidding will be relatively easy. The best trump suit is learned early enough that the partnership can devote the remaining bidding room to other issues, such as:

1. Should we stop in game?
2. Should we be looking for a slam?
3. Should we just bid a slam?

POSTMORTEM

This agreement is one that you need to discuss with your partner. Be aware that opener will always be declarer in a spade contract and responder will always be declarer in a heart contract.

South Deals   +   East-West Vulnerable

	WEST		EAST
♠	Q J 10 9 5	♠	8 3
♥	A Q 9 2	♥	J 8 7 3
♦	K 2	♦	Q J 4
♣	7 3	♣	K Q J 4

WEST	NORTH	EAST	SOUTH
			1♣
1♠	Pass	1NT	Pass
2♥	Pass	?	

SOUTH OPENS 1♣, giving West a choice between bidding 1♠ and doubling. Both bids have modest flaws. If you bid 1♠ you may not be able to show your hearts, but if you double and then bid spades your partner will expect more. He also may bid diamonds, which you don't really want him to do.

1♠ is the better choice. You are lucky in that you get another chance, as so often happens. The next player passes and your partner bids 1NT. This is an important bid. When your partner overcalls and you have ten points, it is likely that your side can make something. East should not miss this chance to bid.

Note that 1NT is not forcing since it is in response to an overcall. West can, if he wishes, pass 1NT.

West has choices. He can pass or he can bid 2♥. I would vote for 2♥ because of the nice suits. The result of this is that East has to answer yet another problem. Should East bid 3♥ or pass?

While East is thinking about this, I have a question for you. How can East know that West has only four hearts? Couldn't West have five spades and five hearts? There's a logical answer.

West has to have five spades and four hearts because if he had five of each, his first bid would be 2♣, Michaels. When you do not use Michaels, you deny a five-five hand.

So East knows that West has only four hearts. East still has to think about raising. I guess that passing is best because East has very little help for West's suits. Some or all of East's high-card points rate to be worthless. Predictably, stopping in 2♥ is best.

QUICKIE

No one is vulnerable. Your LHO opens with 3♥, which is passed to you. What is your best bid?

♠ Q 3
♥ 9 6 2
♦ A K Q 8
♣ K Q 4 3

Pass. All of your bids are dangerous. You shouldn't double without spade support. You can't bid 3NT without a heart stopper. Bidding four of a minor is asking for trouble. If partner doesn't like your suit, it will be messy.

Having a lot of high-card points doesn't mean that you have to bid.

	WEST		EAST
♠	Q 9 8 5 4 2	♠	A
♥	2	♥	K J 8 6
♦	9 7 6 3	♦	K Q 5
♣	J 10	♣	K Q 8 7 2

WEST	NORTH	EAST	SOUTH
	4♥	?	

THIS HAND IS a simple test of your bidding methods and then of your judgment.

East has to pass 4♥. A double of 4♥ is for takeout. This is based on the idea that you will have dozens of takeout double hands for every penalty double hand. If you double 4♥ on this hand and also on the example hand below, your partner won't know what to do.

	WEST		EAST
♠	Q 9 8 5 4 2	♠	K J 6 3
♥	2	♥	4
♦	9 7 6 3	♦	A K 4 2
♣	J 10	♣	K Q 7 3

The great majority of players today play that a double of 4♥ is a takeout double, showing a hand like this one. It has around eighteen support points for all of the unbid suits.

If East does double, West will bid 4♠ with his hand. He is expecting East to have spade support and a good hand and if this is true, the West hand with its six spades is a good hand. In spite of West's weak hand, 4♠ has excellent chances.

But if East makes a penalty double of 4♥ and does not show up with spade support, 4♠ will be down.

Be sure you and your partner are in agreement about this double.

IN A PAIR TOURNAMENT run before they had computers at every table, caddies would pick up the scoring slips and deliver them to the directors in charge of their sections. Late in the session, two caddies were in such a rush to deliver their pickup slips to the scorekeepers that they bumped into each other. Their score slips went up into the air and came down in confusion. Easy to fix, you say? Not if both sections were using the same color pickup slips, green.

South Deals + North-South Vulnerable

WEST	EAST
♠ K J 8 7 4	♠ 2
♥ K Q 4	♥ J 7 6 3
♦ 10 2	♦ K J 9 6 5 4
♣ A J 8	♣ 5 2

WEST	NORTH	EAST	SOUTH
			Pass
1♠	1NT	?	

EAST IS THE hand that has a problem on this auction. West makes a normal 1♠ bid and North overcalls 1NT, showing 15–18 high-card points. In this recurring situation, East has to decide if his hand is worth a bid.

If you play that a 2♦ bid shows a good hand you can't do that. But logically, East should not have a good hand. If he did, he would double 1NT. East should be permitted to bid 2♦ on the hand he has here. It gets East into the auction and it makes life a little harder for South.

The main point of this hand is that East should be able to bid something without fearing that West will not understand what East has.

For the record, there are some conventions that you can use after their 1NT overcall. One possibility is that you play Hamilton over the 1NT bid.

Double is penalty.

2♣ says you have a one-suited hand. It might turn out that you have a raise for partner's suit.

2♦ says you have the majors.

2♥ says you have hearts and a minor.

2♠ says you have spades and a minor.

Given that your side doesn't rate to have a game contract doesn't mean that your side can't have a partscore. This bidding agreement will let you fight for it.

QUICKIE

You open 1♥ and partner makes a limit raise to 3♥, promising at least four-card support. Do you go on to game with this hand?

♠ 4
♥ K J 10 8 5
♦ A K 10 5
♣ J 10 7

Here's a good rule of thumb. If partner makes a limit raise in a major and you have a small singleton somewhere, you should go to game. You won't know how well the hands fit but in general, you will have a play for game. Remember that the opponents don't know what you have so they won't always find the best defense. I won't quote a hand to make a point. You will win some, you will lose some, but in the long run, you will win more often than not.

HAND	WEST	EAST
18	♠ A Q J 8 7 4	♠ 10 5
	♥ 7 6	♥ A K 8 4 2
	♦ 2	♦ A K 10 3
	♣ J 10 7 4	♣ 9 3

WEST	NORTH	EAST	SOUTH
2♠	Pass	2NT	Pass
3♣	Pass	4♠	All pass

WEST OPENS 2♠, weak, and East considers what to do. On this vulnerability, East should think of a game. West rates to have a sane weak two-bid and East has a modest fit plus four certain tricks and a ruffing value.

If your partnership style towards weak two-bids is really sound, I suggest just bidding 4♠ without wasting time asking questions. If you are an aggressive partnership, bidding 2NT to ask opener's opinion is good.

In this case, the 2NT bid asks opener if he has something out-side of spades and at the same time if opener has a maximum.

West doesn't have a maximum in high cards but his suit is good and he has shape. I would compare this hand with others and think that this is closer to a maximum than not. Given this the bid is 3♣, saying that you have something in clubs.

Traditionally this says you have the ace or king. Here, West does not have that but in the interests of expressing his hand he has to make a stronger bid than 3♠, so 3♣ is the default bid. Nuts to rules. Do what is right.

East, finding that West has something extra, makes the reasonable bid of 4♠. West won't make it quickly but in time he may well take ten tricks. Heck, if things work out, he might take eleven tricks.

The big point of this hand is that East really does have game interest. He doesn't have a random fifteen-point hand with one spade. He has something of a fit, which is why he bid this way.

IN THE VERY EARLY DAYS of bridge, some players needed to be reminded what suit was trumps. Hence the invention of Trump Indicators.

These were small devices that could display a spade symbol if spades were trump, a heart symbol for hearts, etc, and a NT symbol when the contract was in notrump. Some rare versions of trump indicators permitted the numbers 1 to 7 too, so that no one would forget what the contract was. These devices did not show the vulnerability. The players were on their own there.

These devices were fanciful and they are a prized collectible for some bridge players. You can see a remarkable selection of these things if you look for trump indicators on the internet.

I have four of them. I know someone who has two hundred.

West Deals   +   No One Vulnerable

WEST	EAST
♠ A K 7 4 3	♠ Q
♥ Q 7	♥ J 8 6 4
♦ J 7 2	♦ K Q 8 5
♣ A 8 2	♣ Q 9 7 5

WEST	NORTH	EAST	SOUTH
1♠	Pass	?	

IF YOU ARE playing a forcing notrump response to one of a major, East will bid 1NT. West will bid something and responder will decide how to continue.

If you are not playing a forcing notrump response, East has a different problem. The question in this article is, what should East bid if not using a forcing notrump response?

Should East still bid 1NT or should he bid something else with his ten-point hand?

WEST	NORTH	EAST	SOUTH
1♠	Pass	1NT	All pass

Some ten-point hands are too good to bid 1NT, but not this one. East should bid 1NT. If opener passes it, it's unlikely that anything will be missed. On this hand opener has a fair fourteen points and he will pass 1NT. East will probably make it, and making 2NT is possible. But I'd rather be in 1NT.

The point of this simple hand is that if 1NT is not forcing, you shouldn't mind bidding 1NT with ten high-card points if no other bid makes sense.

Note that if East had the ♥10, the ♦10, and the ♣10, he would have a much easier time in the play.

West Deals   +   North-South Vulnerable

WEST	EAST
♠ K Q 10 7 6 4	♠ J 9 3
♥ 7	♥ K 8 3 2
♦ A Q 8 7 4	♦ J 10
♣ 2	♣ Q 9 4 3

WEST	NORTH	EAST	SOUTH
1♠	Pass	2♠	Pass
?			

WEST OPENS HIS eleven-point hand with 1♠, a rare case of an opening bid being this light. You have the spade suit and you have super distribution.

When East raises to 2♠, West has to reevaluate his hand in case he wants to bid again.

Would you?

The West hand has only eleven high-card points but it's worth a lot more. My instincts would be to bid 4♠. If you bid 4♠ you will find that dummy has five wasted points in hearts and clubs but game is still possible if you can get to dummy and if the diamond finesse works. If East had the ♣A or the ♦K instead of the ♥K and the ♣Q, game would be that much better.

Note that if you bid 4♠ directly, you may get a diamond lead. If you dabble around and bid 3♦ first, you won't get a diamond lead.

The main point of this hand is that West shouldn't be a point-counter but should appreciate the value of his shape and then should further appreciate how much the hand goes up in value when East raises.

South Deals + East-West Vulnerable

	WEST		EAST
♠	A 8	♠	J 9
♥	Q J 4	♥	K 7 3 2
♦	Q 8 4	♦	J 10 7
♣	K Q J 8 3	♣	A 7 6 2

WEST	NORTH	EAST	SOUTH
			3♠
?			

IF THERE WAS one skill I would like to be able to teach, it would be judgment.

Judgment is an accumulation of experience where you see how a particular bid works out and then file it away for future reference. After playing enough hands, you should have a huge accumulation of information you can draw on. Some players are gifted with the ability to use this information. Some are not. I think it is similar to learning a language. Some people are gifted with language skills. Some (me) are not.

Take the West hand here. Your RHO opens 3♠ and you have this fifteen-point hand that might have opened with 1NT.

What should you bid over 3♠?

The correct bid in the long run is pass. Yes, you have a full opening bid but you have no shape and many of your values are soft.

Your choices are 3NT and double. If you bid 3NT, you better find partner with a good hand. And if you double, you risk ending in a four-three heart fit. This is not automatically bad but with no shape to speak of, playing in a four-three fit is not ideal.

On this hand, 4♥ would be the contract if you doubled, and this has no play even with good luck. With normal breaks, 4♥ would be down a few, and you do not expect good luck. The preempt warned you that things will not break well for you.

Note that your partner actually has a fair hand. He has eight working points along with the wasted ♠J.

Note also that even if you find the best trump suit, clubs, your fit is so bad that you are not safe there either.

RULE

There is no disgrace in passing when you have a good hand. I hate it and so should you, but it is possible that passing may be best. Don't let passing be your default mood, however. Be aware that winning bridge is aggressive bridge. Just be careful to be aggressive at the right time.

POSTMORTEM

I mentioned that double and 3NT were the only two sensible bids. There's another bid that some would consider. It's 4♣. This is a terrible bid for many reasons. Here are some of them.

1. You need partner to have a good hand if you are to come close to making 4♣. If he doesn't have it, you go down. This will be especially bad if someone doubles.
2. If partner has enough that you can make 4♣, he will have a good enough hand to raise to 5♣.
3. There are hands where 3NT will make and 4♣ won't.
4. Some fifteen-point hands are worth bidding with. This is a lousy fifteen points which has three queens, two jacks, and poor distribution.

West Deals   +   Both Sides Vulnerable

	WEST	EAST	

	WEST	EAST
♠	A 10 8 6	♠ 7 2
♥	A Q 7 6	♥ J 10 8 5 4
♦	3	♦ J 8 6 2
♣	A K 7 3	♣ Q 8

WEST	NORTH	EAST	SOUTH
1♣	Pass	?	

THIS DISCUSSION IS one of the most important I have ever written about. It covers a common situation that many players are not aware of. Read this discussion more than once.

Look at the East hand. Should East respond to West's 1♣? Some players are willing to respond with very little and some prefer to have the six points, which is considered normal.

Would you bid 1♥ or pass?

WEST	NORTH	EAST	SOUTH
1♣	Pass	Pass	1♦
Dbl	Pass	?	

Passing 1♣ is probably right because you aren't prepared to hear your partner rebid 1♠. For a second there, you were close to playing in 1♣. The auction continues as shown and East gets a second chance to bid. South's bid has given your side an opportunity to look further.

How do you feel about this? You don't have much of a hand and the ♦J is wasted, but you do have some useful values. What do you bid in response to partner's double? Explain.

WEST	NORTH	EAST	SOUTH
1♣	Pass	Pass	1♦
Dbl	Pass	2♥	Pass
4♥	All pass		

Did you think of bidding 2♥? If so, you made a fine bid that was overlooked when this hand was played at the table.

You should be very pleased with the way this auction has gone. By passing originally, you limited your hand. When you jumped to 2♥, you told your partner that you have as good a hand as you can have under the circumstances.

BOX PRINCIPLE

In my book *Hand Evaluation*, the most difficult book I ever wrote, I introduced the concept of the Box Principle. It is simple to understand and simple to use.

It works like this:

When you make a bid, your partner will often know your hand within a tight range. Here are some examples.

WEST	NORTH	EAST	SOUTH
1♣	Pass	1NT	

East shows eight to ten points.

WEST	NORTH	EAST	SOUTH
1♣	Pass	Pass	

East shows zero to five points.

WEST	NORTH	EAST	SOUTH
1♣	Pass	1♥	Pass
1NT			

West shows twelve to fourteen points.

RULE

If you make a bid and your partner invites you to go on, you look at your hand and ask yourself this question.

Given what I am known to have, do I have a maximum or a minimum?

On the hand above, East showed a bad hand when he passed 1♣ but when West followed with a takeout double, East knew he had a great hand under the circumstances. His jump to 2♥ said he had a maximum in the box of hands that included zero to five points. I judge that the East hand is worth seven points after West's double. East knows West has hearts for his double. East counts three points for the ♥J and the ♣Q, and adds one point because they are good cards. East adds a point for having five hearts. East adds a couple of points for having two doubletons. East does not count the ♦J.

West knows what East has and his 4♥ bid said that he did not need much from East. Looking at the combined hands, you can see that ten tricks are cold and eleven are possible. I wonder what South is thinking now. He had a chance to defend against 1♣ and now he is defending against a cold game.

The world uses the Box Principle already. They just do not know how extensive it is.

Say you play 20–21 point 2NT openers. You open 2NT with an average twenty-count and your partner bids 4NT asking you to bid six with a maximum and to pass with a minimum.

You routinely look at your twenty points and you calculate that as 2NT openers go, this one is minimum. And you pass, unless you enjoy playing in bad slams.

Remember: Do not evaluate your hand in terms of how you like it, evaluate your hand in terms of whether you have a good hand or a bad hand for the bids you have made so far.

North Deals + No One Vulnerable

EAST

♠ 10 8 7 5
♥ 10 8 2
♦ A Q 9 4
♣ Q 4

WEST	NORTH	EAST	SOUTH
	1♥	Pass	Pass
2NT	Pass	?	

EAST HAS A poor hand but the auction goes in a way that should get his attention.

Do you know what West's 2NT shows?

What should East bid?

WEST	NORTH	EAST	SOUTH
	1♥	Pass	Pass
2NT	Pass	3♣	Pass
3♦	Pass	3NT	All pass

West's 2NT bid shows a nice eighteen up to a modest twenty high-card points. It is a natural bid, not unusual. There are two reasons for not playing 2NT as unusual.

One. If West has the minors, he should wonder where the major suits are. East didn't bid over 1♥ so he may be weak in spades. It is not impossible that North-South can make a spade contract. Bidding 2NT to show the minors is likely to give their side a second chance at finding a spade fit.

This is a real danger, not a theoretical one.

The second reason is that using 2NT to show 18–20 high-card points with hearts stopped makes the bidding easy for your side.

	WEST		EAST
♠	A Q 6	♠	10 8 7 5
♥	A K 7	♥	10 8 2
♦	10 5 2	♦	A Q 9 4
♣	A K 10 7	♣	Q 4

POSTMORTEM

You can use Stayman, Jacoby, and Texas when partner bids 2NT. East might have just raised to 3NT but his Stayman bid was reasonable.

East Deals   +   No One Vulnerable

WEST

♠ Q 9 7 6
♥ 7
♦ A 5 2
♣ 9 8 5 4 2

WEST	NORTH	EAST	SOUTH
		2♣	Pass
?			

EAST OPENS 2♣, and that should interest West. If East has a notrump hand, game will be high enough, but if East can bid any suit other than hearts, this West hand will be interested in a slam.

For the moment, what should West bid?

WEST	NORTH	EAST	SOUTH
		2♣	Pass
2♦	Pass	2♥	Pass
?			

West should bid 2♦. This is a waiting bid. I have decided after much soul-searching that 2♦ should be bid with just about any hand. Even if you have a nice suit and a few points, bidding your suit tends to get in opener's way. I almost always bid 2♦ to see what my partner has. Very seldom have I regretted doing this.

East's 2♥ rebid is not unexpected but it's a disappointment for West, who had hoped for almost anything else.

How should West continue? Do you have a plan?

WEST	NORTH	EAST	SOUTH
		2♣	Pass
2♦	Pass	2♥	Pass
2NT	Pass	3♦	Pass
?			

There is a convention you can use here which has gained in popularity. It is called the second negative. It works this way. When your partner opens 2♣ and rebids two of a major, a 3♣ bid by you shows a terrible hand. If your partner has bid 3♣, you would bid 3♦ to show the bad hand. If your partner's rebid was 3♦, you would bid 3♥ or 3NT (depending on which your partnership prefers) to show a bad hand.

This hand is actually pretty good. It is too good to bid 3♣, because that would be interpreted as showing a poor hand.

I have West bidding 2NT. This shows anything from four good points up to the moon. It is natural and forcing to game.

When East bids 3♦, West has a new situation. He has two bids to consider, 4♦ and 3NT. What would you bid?

WEST	NORTH	EAST	SOUTH
		2♣	Pass
2♦	Pass	2♥	Pass
2NT	Pass	3♦	Pass
3NT	Pass	4♣	Pass
?			

West did bid 3NT. It wasn't a comfortable choice. The reason he didn't raise diamonds is that it is generally wrong to raise partner's second suit with just three trumps. East may have four diamonds and will bid in the expectation that you have four. This is a serious guideline.

East's 4♣ bid is something unexpected. What could it mean? Do you think it is natural or might it be Gerber, asking for aces?

I know that some players play 4♣ is Gerber no matter how the bidding goes and I vote that to be one of the worst agreements imaginable. If you play 4♣ is Gerber, it means you can never bid 4♣ naturally, and that's a big loss. East's 4♣ bid shows clubs and also implies his actual distribution.

What ought West to bid over 4♣?

WEST	NORTH	EAST	SOUTH
		2♣	Pass
2♦	Pass	2♥	Pass
2NT	Pass	3♦	Pass
3NT	Pass	4♣	Pass
6♣	All pass		

This is a little bit of a prayer, but it's a fair one. You have an ace, which is super, and you have five-card support. By now you know your partner is void in spades so the odds are that you are closer to making 7♣ than five. I am settling on 6♣ because it rates to make and because I can't see a way to bid seven safely.

WEST	EAST
♠ Q976	♠ –
♥ 7	♥ AKQ42
♦ A52	♦ KQJ6
♣ 98542	♣ AQJ10

Note that if you bid 5♣, a conservative action, your partner will be unsure that it is safe to go on. Taking the bull by the horns looks best.

In fact, you are in a cold contract with a play for seven. Be happy to have reached a good small slam.

Earlier in this hand I discussed what 2♦ showed and suggested it's best to bid only 2♦ no matter what you have.

Say you had a slightly better hand and decided to let partner know you have some points by responding 2NT instead of 2♦.

He will have to bid 3♥ and then will have to decide what to do next. It will be impossible for him to bid all three suits without getting dangerously high.West's 2NT bid has taken away a lot of useful bidding space.

Special thought: East's opening bid of 2♣ would be popular but as you saw, it was responsible for an awkward auction. When you have 5-4-4-0 shape or 4-4-4-1 shape, you should consider opening with one of a suit. But there's always a risk. If you opened the East hand with 1♥, it might be passed out. Still, for any shapely hand that is a borderline 2♣ bid, starting with one of a suit is often a good idea.

East Deals + North-South Vulnerable

WEST

♠ J 9 7 3 2
♥ 8 6 3
♦ 4
♣ Q 10 8 7

WEST	NORTH	EAST	SOUTH
		1♦	

WHAT DO YOU think of the West hand? Initially, it looks pretty awful. It's nice that partner could open but this hand really doesn't have much to offer at this point.

WEST	NORTH	EAST	WEST
		1♦	Dbl
?			

South doubles 1♦. Should you bid something? Other than passing, a 1♠ bid is the only thing that comes to mind here.

What would a 1♠ bid by West mean?

I've discussed this topic in multiple articles in multiple publications and have written a book about it. It's an important topic. A brief summary is that bidding a new suit at the one level over a takeout double is the same as if there had been no takeout double. If you choose to bid 1♠, your partner will treat the bid as forcing and will make the same rebids that he would normally make. If you bid, your partner will expect a better hand. There's a lot of room for trouble. West should pass. Some play that a 1♠ bid is weak. That's bad for many reasons. Save your bids here for hands where you have something to say.

The auction continues thusly:

WEST	NORTH	EAST	SOUTH
		1♦	Dbl
Pass	1♥	Dbl	2♥
?			

Your hands wasn't worth a bid at the one level. Is it worth a bid at the two level?

Having passed, your partner thinks you have a weak hand. Well, you do. But in light of partner's takeout double, you have a very good hand.

The West hand is not only worth 2♠, it is worth thinking about bidding 3♠. If you flirted with a 3♠ bid, you get a modest nod of approval from here.

WEST	NORTH	EAST	SOUTH
		1♦	Dbl
Pass	1♥	Dbl	2♥
2♠	All pass		

Here's the layout:

	WEST		EAST
♠	J 9 7 3 2	♠	A K 5
♥	8 6 3	♥	10
♦	4	♦	A J 10 6 3
♣	Q 10 8 7	♣	A 6 4 2

East did some good things. He made a takeout double of 1♥. Some would bid 2♣ or 2♦, both pretty awful bids. Double is far better because it keeps all three suits in the game. Those clubs don't look so hot that I'd want to mention them if I can find a better bid.

Having made a takeout double, East made a fine bid by passing 2♠. East has a good double but he has only three spades. If East had a fourth spade, he could raise to 3♠, a mildly pushy bid. East should recall that West did not bid over the double. West's hand, whatever it is, should be pretty weak. One more point in the bidding. West's hand is good enough that if East (on a different hand) were to raise to 3♠, West should bid game.

| | HAND | North Deals + No One Vulnerable |

HAND 26

	WEST	EAST
♠	8 7 4	♠ –
♥	Q 10 8 7 5 3	♥ A J 9 2
♦	A J 6	♦ K 8 7 2
♣	3	♣ A K Q J 5

WEST	NORTH	EAST	SOUTH
	3♠	Dbl	4♠
5♥	Pass	6♥	All pass

NORTH OPENS 3♠ and East has a very nice takeout double. South pushes on to 4♠, giving West a decision. West could make the claim that, "I only had seven points, partner," but that would be a lame excuse for passing. West does have only seven points but he has six hearts, an ace, and a singleton club. I would not pass this hand on this sequence on any vulnerability.

East must appreciate how good his hand is in light of the bidding. It is true that slam may not be cold, but West did bid at the five level. If he has five hearts to the KQ, slam will have a play.

This is the kind of hand that separates players with a conservative stance from players who are willing to take chances. If you think about it, I bet that the consistent winners in your group are the ones who take chances, as long as they are sane chances.

If you do bid 6♥ you will make just six, losing a trick to South's ♥K.

It turns out that they should have bid 6♠. North can take nine tricks in a spade contract.

North Deals　+　North-South Vulnerable

	WEST		EAST
♠	K 10 9 8 2	♠	6
♥	J	♥	A Q 9 5 4 2
♦	K 7 5 4	♦	A J 10
♣	J 3 2	♣	K Q 5

WEST	NORTH	EAST	SOUTH
	Pass	1♥	1♠
Pass	Pass	?	

EAST OPENED 1♥ and South overcalled 1♠. This was passed back to East, who is obviously going to bid again. The question is which bid he should make. Do you have a clear choice?

WEST	NORTH	EAST	SOUTH
	Pass	1♥	1♠
Pass	Pass	Dbl	All pass

East does well to double. If West has a penalty pass, East has enough values that South will be down a lot. If West does not have a penalty pass and bids something, East will probably end up in 2♥. The difference between doubling and bidding 2♥ is that the double can gain a lot. On this hand South will go down two tricks for 500, much better than East could have done by playing the hand.

The key to choosing double is that East has enough defensive
strength to compensate for his having extra distribution.

♠ 2
♥ K Q J 10 8 3
♦ K 8 3
♣ A 6 3

he would bid 2♥. If East had:

♠ 2
♥ A Q J 8 7 6 3
♦ A K 3
♣ J 8

he would bid 3♥. If East had:

♠ 2
♥ K Q J 8 3
♦ K Q 10 9 7
♣ Q 5

he would bid 2♦. If East had:

♠ –
♥ A Q J 9 8 4
♦ K 3
♣ A Q 10 7 5

he would bid 3♣. This shows a big, shapely hand that isn't
quite worth an opening 2♣ bid. Partner can pass 3♣ if he has a

wretched hand and can give a preference to 3♥, which opener should tend to pass.

If East had:

♠ K Q 8
♥ K J 8 5 4
♦ K 4 3
♣ Q 7

he would pass. A 1NT bid should show more than an opening 1NT bid. Eighteen or nineteen points is about right. West, remember, didn't bid over 1♠. He is likely to have a weak hand.

North Deals   +   North-South Vulnerable

WEST	EAST
♠ 3	♠ A J 8 7 4
♥ 6	♥ K Q 8 7 3
♦ K 10 9 7 6 5 3	♦ 8
♣ K 7 6 3	♣ 10 7

WEST	NORTH	EAST	SOUTH
	1♦	2♦	Dbl
All pass			

HERE'S A HAND to test your understandings and your courage. North opens 1♦ and East makes a Michaels cuebid showing both majors. South doubles. Looking at the West hand, would you not agree that all things being equal, 2♦ doubled is probably the least-bad contract your side has?

How do you get that message over to partner?

The answer all comes down to agreements.

Here is a suggestion that you will thank me for some day.

When your partner bids Michaels and is doubled, a pass by you says you want to play right here. If you pass, partner should pass too.

If you want to play in a major suit, you either bid it or you redouble if you have the same number of cards in both majors and want partner to choose.

Finally, if you wish to play in the unbid minor, just bid it. Your partner will know that you are aware of his majors and he will know you hate them.

You may end up being set a bunch, but you should be able to make that bunch as small as possible.

North Deals + No One Vulnerable

WEST

- ♠ 7
- ♥ K Q 7 3
- ♦ Q J 8 4
- ♣ A 10 6 3

WEST	NORTH	EAST	SOUTH
	1♠	Pass	1NT*
?			

NORTH-SOUTH ARE USING Two Over One methods so that 1NT bid by South is forcing. Usually a forcing notrump looks just like any other 1NT response and includes five to nine high-card points. About one time in ten the notrump bidder has more. This can happen when he has a limit raise with three-card support, or when he has an eleven-point notrump-type hand. In both of these cases, South intends to make a strong bid on his next turn.

Should West be cautious or should he bid? If South has eleven points, getting into the bidding could be a bad idea.

WEST	NORTH	EAST	SOUTH
	1♠	Pass	1NT
Dbl	Pass	2♥	2♠
?			

West correctly doubles. This is for takeout and essentially says West would have doubled a 1♠ opening bid for takeout had he had the chance. There isn't one iota of penalty in the definition of this double. Yes, South could have a good hand. Experience says that if you have a correct double, you should go ahead and double and not worry about South's possible good hands.

East bids 2♥ and South bids 2♠, something he might have done earlier. Should West raise hearts?

West should pass. He made a takeout double and has just what he said he had. If anyone should bid 3♥ (or 3♣ or 3♦), it is East.

WEST	NORTH	EAST	SOUTH
	1♠	Pass	1NT
Dbl	Pass	2♥	2♠
Pass	Pass	Dbl	Pass
?			

East isn't done. East doubles 2♠, giving West something new to think about. What should West do?

West should pass the double.

Think about the bidding. South didn't raise spades immediately. Normally when you have three-card support for a major, it is best to raise. South's bidding suggests he has only two spades and a smattering of points.

If South has two spades, how many does your partner have?

East probably as five of them. Your partner's double says he has good spades and some values. West should pass.

WEST	EAST
♠ 7	♠ K Q 9 6 4
♥ K Q 7 3	♥ J 10 8 5
♦ Q J 8 4	♦ 9 2
♣ A 10 6 3	♣ Q 7

East's hand is par for this bidding. He has five spades with some good spot cards. His ♠9 is a big card defensively. East would be slower to double holding ♠K6543.

West's original double is totally for takeout, a point I made and repeated above. Here is a trap that West should avoid. If this was West's hand, he should not double.

WEST

♠ A J 2
♥ 4 2
♦ A K J 2
♣ K J 6 5

This hand has seventeen points but it doesn't have heart support. You cannot double with this because your partner will bid 2♥ more often than not. Sure, you can bid 2NT over that, but that will just get you in even deeper.

Your LHO has an opening bid and your RHO has, on the average, seven or eight points. This means their side has twenty or so.

Adding and subtracting brings you to the conclusion that your partner has three points on a good day.

Your hand is worth an opening 1NT. If you end up in 2NT, it's the equivalent of your opening 1NT and somehow reaching 2NT facing three points. Not realistic. It is much better to defend when you have a balanced hand.

West Deals + Both Sides Vulnerable

WEST	EAST
♠ 2	♠ K J 7 4
♥ Q 8 2	♥ 9 4
♦ K 8 5	♦ Q 9 6
♣ A Q J 6 5 2	♣ K 8 4 3

WEST	NORTH	EAST	SOUTH
1♣	Pass	1♠	Pass
2♣	Pass	?	

AN EASY HAND. West bids 1♣ and East responds 1♠. No big deal here. The only question is what to do when West rebids 2♣.

Should East bid something or should he pass?

East should raise to 3♣. This is for two reasons. There is an outside chance that your side can make something, perhaps 3NT. And, there is a fair expectation that if partner is minimum, the opponents will get together and bid something.

Raising to 3♣ addresses both concerns.

WEST	NORTH	EAST	SOUTH
1♣	Pass	1♠	Pass
2♣	Pass	3♣	All pass

3♣ isn't cold. If you are unlucky, you could lose five tricks. However, 3♣, making or going down a trick, is better than having your opponents bid 3♥, which would make three or four depending on how well declarer guesses the hand.

East Deals + Both Sides Vulnerable

WEST	EAST
♠ Q J 8 7	♠ 10 6 5 2
♥ Q 7	♥ 9 4
♦ K Q 7 2	♦ A 8 6
♣ A Q 8	♣ K J 5 3

WEST	NORTH	EAST	SOUTH
1NT	2♣	?	

WEST STARTS WITH a strong notrump and North overcalls 2♣. In today's world, a 2♣ bid may or may not show clubs. He may have both majors (Landy), he may have clubs and a higher suit (DONT), he may have hearts and a minor (Astro), and he may have an unknown one-suited hand (Hamilton/Cappelletti).

East has enough to bid over 2♣. Should he make different bids according to what the 2♣ bid means, or is there a single bid that will work no matter what the 2♣ bid means?

For better or for worse, there is a very reasonable treatment you should consider. When your RHO bids 2♣, use a double as Stayman and use 2♦ and 2♥ as transfer bids.

If the overcall is 2♦ you can double to show a Stayman hand, but transfer bids don't apply.

WEST	NORTH	EAST	SOUTH
1NT	2♣	Dbl	Pass
2♠	3♥	?	

West showed four spades, which is good news. You have a fit. North's 3♥ bid can mean a number of things, and you should ask what it is. Let's assume that he has a one-suited hand with hearts. This is the most likely explanation for North's bidding.

What should East bid over 3♥?

WEST	NORTH	EAST	SOUTH
1NT	2♣	Dbl	Pass
2♠	3♥	3♠	All pass

Raise to 3♠. This is invitational, just as if the bidding had gone on without any competitive bidding.

For those of you who use 2♣ overcalls to show a one-suited hand, this hand is an example of why the convention isn't effective. East was able to bid Stayman and the partnership got to a nice 3♠ contract. Had North overcalled 2♥, natural, it would have caused more problems than 2♣.

North's 2♣ bid left East room to do all the things he wanted to do.

POSTMORTEM

Let's face it. If an opponent bids over your partner's 1NT opening, it can make life difficult. Using a double of 2♣ as Stayman and 2♦ and 2♥ as Jacoby transfers is useful.

And, using a double of 2♦ as Stayman is useful too.

West Deals   +   North-South Vulnerable

	WEST	EAST	
♠	K 10 3	♠ J 8 4	
♥	A Q J 8 7	♥ 10	
♦	Q 8	♦ 9 7 6 5 2	
♣	A Q J	♣ K 6 5 2	

WEST	NORTH	EAST	SOUTH
1♥	1♠	Pass	Pass
?			

WEST WAS GETTING ready to jump to 2NT but the auction didn't go as planned. What should West rebid after North's 1♠ bid is passed back to him?

WEST	NORTH	EAST	SOUTH
1♥	1♠	Pass	Pass
1NT	All pass		

West can bid 1NT and do justice to his hand. It's all logical. Here is the reasoning.

If West had twelve to fourteen points, he wouldn't bid this way because it would be dangerous to bid when East is potentially weak.

If West had fifteen to seventeen points, he might have opened 1NT. Some partnerships will open 1NT with a five-card major. It's not a bad idea.

Only if West has eighteen or nineteen, and intended to rebid 2NT over a one-level response from partner, is it safe to bid 1NT facing a hand that could be useless.

This bid ends the auction and as you can see, it leads to a contract that is not cold. If 1NT is in danger, you do not want to be higher.

POSTMORTEM

West avoided doubling 1♠. If he did that, East would bid his diamonds and West would probably bid 2NT, most likely going down.

QUICKIE

♠ 3 2
♥ K J 3 2
♦ Q J 10 7
♣ 7 6 2

♠ A 5
♥ A Q 10 8 4
♦ A K 9 2
♣ A 4

This hand offers something to think about. What contract do you want to be in?

You can't make 6NT. There are eleven tricks.

You can't make 6♥, either. The same eleven tricks.

However, 6♦, while not cold, is a very good contract. If diamonds are 3-2, 6♦ is easy. Draw trump, run hearts, discarding dummy's small spade, and ruff a spade in dummy. Even if diamonds are 4-1, you will probably make 6♦ unless the defenders specifically lead a spade.

The message? A 4-4 fit often provides an extra trick.

North Deals   +   East-West Vulnerable

WEST	EAST
♠ 2	♠ A J 9 5
♥ K J 9 6 4 2	♥ 8 3
♦ Q 6 3	♦ A K J
♣ J 3 2	♣ Q 9 8 6

WEST	NORTH	EAST	SOUTH
	4♠	?	

WHEN NORTH OPENED 4♠, East must have thought it was Christmas. How can East get the most out of this hand? What should he bid to get that result?

WEST	NORTH	EAST	SOUTH
	4♠	All pass	

The answer depends on your methods. If you play a double of 4♠ is for penalty, you can do that. Experience has shown that this is not the best method. Better is to use double as takeout.

Do you know why double is best used for takeout?

The reason is one of frequency. If you think about it, you are more likely to have a hand that wants to make a takeout double than one that wants to make a penalty double.

♠ 2
♥ A Q J 8
♦ K J 3 2
♣ A Q 8 3

When an opponent opens 4♠, he usually has a good suit. You won't often have lots of spade tricks. More likely you will have a hand like the one above.

Since you will have many more good hands that want to make a takeout double than a penalty double, it's wise to use double to cover the frequent hands.

Can I hear someone saying that 4NT can be used for takeout? That is nonsense. Here's why.

1.   ♠ 3
                   ♥ 2
                   ♦ A K J 7 3
                   ♣ A K 10 9 7 3

2.   ♠ 7
                   ♥ A K 3 2
                   ♦ A K 8 3
                   ♣ Q 8 3 2

Let's face it. Every player in the world would bid 4NT with the first hand to show the minors. This is normal good bridge.

Now, if it is right to bid 4NT with the first hand, how can you bid 4NT with the second hand and expect your partner to know which hand you have?

It can't be done.

Playing double for takeout offers a possible bonus.

If you choose to play that double is for takeout, your partner may have a hand that looks better suited for defense than for play and if he chooses to pass your double, you may still get a penalty.

POSTMORTEM

Look at the original hand at the top of this discussion. If East doubles for penalty and West thinks double is for takeout, West might bid 5♥. That would turn a triumph into a disaster.

West Deals   +   North-South Vulnerable

	WEST		EAST
♠	A K 10 6 4 3	♠	7
♥	A K	♥	J 8 4
♦	Q 3	♦	A 7 6 2
♣	A Q 8	♣	K J 9 6 3

WEST	NORTH	EAST	SOUTH
2♣	Pass	3♣	Pass
3♠	Pass	3NT	Pass
4♣	Pass	4♦	Pass
6♣	All pass		

WEST HAS A big one and starts with 2♣. The entire key to this hand is what East does over 2♣. If East bids 3♣, as he should with his nice hand and his good five-card suit, a slam will be reached. If East responds with 2♦, he will never be able to show his clubs. Look what happens if East bids 2♦. West will rebid 2♠ and East will have to bid.... oops. If East bids 3♣, it is the second negative showing a hopeless hand and saying nothing about clubs. East just can't bid his clubs now. East can bid notrump perhaps, but that also leads nowhere. West will bid spades some more or may raise notrump, but the club slam will be buried in a morass of unfortunate system.

Note that while 6♣ is a decent slam and 7♣ is makeable against some layouts, a spade slam or a notrump slam is in trouble. Don't ever lose sight of minor suit contracts. Yes, I know that majors and notrump pay more than clubs and diamonds, but only if you make your contract.

South Deals + East-West Vulnerable

WEST		EAST	
♠ Q J 6 3		♠ K 10 8 7 6	
♥ 3		♥ 8 2	
♦ A K Q J 6		♦ 5 2	
♣ A J 7		♣ K 10 4 2	

WEST	NORTH	EAST	SOUTH
			Pass
1♦	4♥	Pass	Pass
Dbl	Pass	4♠	All pass

THE POINT OF this hand is that North's 4♥ bid forced East-West to do some guessing.

East can't bid but West has a good enough hand to keep bidding.

West does best by doubling. This is clearly a takeout double. You will have 25 hands which have shape and values, like this hand, before you have one hand where you know you want to double 4♥ for penalty. Good bidding caters to the hands that do come up.

East, knowing the double is takeout, is very pleased with this. He has five good spades and the ♣K. Since he might have nothing at all, East views this as an excellent hand under the circumstances. East bids 4♠ and plays it there. Most likely, East will make an overtrick.

East Deals + No One Vulnerable

WEST	EAST
♠ 9 3	♠ A J 5 4 2
♥ 9 6 3	♥ 7
♦ 9 4	♦ K Q 5 3
♣ K 10 7 4 3 2	♣ A Q 6

WEST	NORTH	EAST	SOUTH
		1♠	Pass
?			

SHOULD WEST BID something here?

West should pass. If he bids something, he may be faced with an assortment of strong bids from East. West will hate most of them. Say West bids 1NT, an awful bid. What will West bid if East jumps to 3♠? West will pass and watch as East goes down a trick or two.

WEST	NORTH	EAST	SOUTH
		1♠	Pass
Pass	2♥	Dbl	3♥
?			

The auction has taken an interesting turn. The West hand was not worth a response to 1♠ but now that a second opportunity has arisen, West can reconsider. This is a recurring theme in bridge. An apparently poor hand suddenly becomes a good hand.

What did you think the West had was worth when East opened 1♠?

Initially, the West hand might have been worth three or four points if East liked the ♣K. The hand might also be worthless if the ♣K is no good.

What do you think the West hand is worth now that your partner has made a takeout double of 2♥?

East's double is asking you to bid a suit. Your hand has grown enormously. I would value the West hand at nearly nine points. It has only three high-card points but it has two useful doubletons, a super card in clubs, and it has a six-card suit.

Does this add up to enough to bid with and if so, what should West bid?

WEST	NORTH	EAST	SOUTH
		1♠	Pass
Pass	2♥	Dbl	3♥
4♣	All pass		

POSTMORTEM

West bids 4♣ and probably makes it. Against boring defense, he might make five. Against good defense, he should make four. Importantly, if West does not bid 4♣, East-West will defend against 3♥, and that will probably make.

Note that East doesn't bid again when West bids 4♣. East has only to remember that West did pass originally so he can't have more than what he does have. If East had one more club, he could consider bidding again.

East Deals + North-South Vulnerable

WEST

♠ 10 7 6 5 3 2
♥ 2
♦ 9 3
♣ A 9 8 3

WEST	NORTH	EAST	SOUTH
		1♥	Pass
?			

WEST HAS TO decide whether to bid 1♠ or pass in response to 1♥. What is your style?

WEST	NORTH	EAST	SOUTH
		1♥	Pass
1♠	Pass	3♠	Pass
?			

Bidding is right for many reasons. Even though you have a weak hand, your shape suggests a chance that the hand belongs to your side. At the least, you can rebid spades in a pinch.

Another reason to bid is that you cast a spell on the opponents. It is not as if you are going to terrorize them but if you bid, you give them the mindset that they are competing for a partscore, not for a game. I can recall too many hands where I passed a marginal hand like this one and seconds later found myself on lead against 3NT. Had I bid, it probably would have deterred them.

Having bid 1♠, you got lucky. Your partner has spade support and has invited you to bid a game. Do you accept?

Yes, you accept. For the second hand in a row, you have a chance to reevaluate a small hand in terms of new information. This one is now worth about ten points. It has only four high-card points but the singleton and the doubleton are working full time now and your fifth and sixth trumps add important value. Bid game and fully expect it to be cold. Here's the layout:

WEST	EAST
♠ 10 7 6 5 3 2	♠ K Q J 4
♥ 2	♥ A 10 8 7 3
♦ 9 3	♦ A 8 2
♣ A 9 8 3	♣ 4

POSTMORTEM

Even if the defenders lead trumps, you have a play for five by setting up the long heart. As long as you start on hearts before burning all of your dummy entries, you ought to get out for one spade and one diamond loser.

Be sure you appreciate the value of a long suit when a fit becomes known.

Say the bidding had been different. Say your partner opened 1♥ and rebid 2♥ over 1♠. You would pass this and if asked how much your hand was worth, you would think not much.

The singleton heart is worthless, and so is the doubleton diamond. Partner isn't likely to get to ruff a diamond in your hand. And, of course, the value of your long spade suit is zero if the hand is played in hearts.

One last point. Note East's 3♠ rebid. He has fourteen high-card points but they are sensational points. All of his high cards are good. His shape is excellent. East's hand is worth around seventeen points in support of spades. After both East and West reevaluate their hands, they end up in a successful game contract with only eighteen combined high-card points.

HAND 38

WEST	EAST
♠ 8 7 6 3	♠ 5 2
♥ A Q 9 4	♥ K J 2
♦ 2	♦ K Q J 6 3
♣ 8 7 6 2	♣ A 5 3

WEST	NORTH	EAST	SOUTH
		1♦	Pass
1♥	Pass	?	

THIS IS A story hand.

This hand was played at many tables in a local duplicate. At all tables, the bidding started as shown.

What do you think East should rebid over 1♥?

WEST	NORTH	EAST	SOUTH
		1♦	Pass
1♥	Pass	2♥	All pass

At some tables, East rebid his nice diamonds. This contract had no chance and went down at least one trick at all tables. Diamonds divided normally so it wasn't bad breaks that defeated 2♦. The problem was that 2♦ wasn't a good contract.

At some tables, East rebid 1NT. This too failed when the defenders led spades. Declarer had seven tricks but the defense got theirs first. Down one was actually a little lucky since clubs divided three-three. If they were four-two, 1NT would have been down another.

At a few tables, East raised to 2♥, a bid that would not occur to quite a few players. Declarer had little trouble with this contract.

A principle as important as this one can't be proved on the basis of one hand. I have to ask you to trust me on this one.

Here is my guideline:

If I have a normal opening bid, I will raise my partner with three-card support around a third of the time.

Here are a few example hands to show you my thoughts in action.

WEST	NORTH	EAST	SOUTH
		1♦	Pass
1♥	Pass	?	

♠ A 7 6
♥ Q J 3
♦ A Q 5 4 2
♣ 7 2

If you raise to 2♥, you still have ways to get to 3NT if that is best. It may be, however, that a four-three heart fit is your best trump suit. I've seen lots of games and a few slams that can only be successful if played in such a fit. As you saw in the hand in the first paragraph, just getting to a partscore in hearts may be best. Your partner will frequently pass 1NT when he has five so-so hearts and the best fit will be missed.

♠ 7 6 4
♥ A Q 10
♦ A K J 7
♣ 6 5 3

I would raise to 2♥ with this one, too. I do not wish to rebid 1NT and have the opening lead come up to my hand.

♠ Q 8 3
♥ A K 3
♦ Q 8 7 3
♣ K 8 3

This is a 1NT rebid because you have stoppers and aren't unhappy to play in notrump.

This is a genuinely important concept and if you refuse to consider it, a world of good contracts will be unavailable to you.

Here is one layout to show you a four-three fit in action. Look at the two hands and determine the best contract. West is the dealer and opens 1♦.

♠ 8 7	♠ 10 6 2
♥ K J 3	♥ A Q 5 2
♦ A K J 9 8	♦ Q 6
♣ J 7 3	♣ A 10 6 2

3NT is a candidate but it will go down if the opponents can take five spade tricks.

5♦ looks good until you count your tricks. There are exactly ten, no more, no less.

In hearts you have ten tricks, and that's the game you want to play in.

Honestly now. Can you see a way to bid to 4♥ other than having West open 1♦ and raise 1♥ to 2♥?

<table>
<tr><td rowspan="2">**HAND**

39</td><td colspan="3">East Deals + Both Sides Vulnerable</td></tr>
</table>

| HAND 39 | East Deals | + | Both Sides Vulnerable |

	WEST	EAST
♠	3	J 8 6
♥	K 9 7 3	A Q J 10 5 2
♦	Q J 8 7 5 2	K 4
♣	J 3	10 8

WEST	NORTH	EAST	SOUTH
		2♥	Pass
4♥			

THIS HAND DEMONSTRATES one of my favorite rules. If your partner opens with a weak two-bid in a major suit and the next player passes, then…

- If you have four or more trumps
- If you have a singleton
- If you don't think you should look for slam

…you should jump to game (on any vulnerability) and put extra pressure on your opponents. On this hand, East opens a maximum vulnerable weak two-bid in hearts. West, following my rule, jumps to 4♥. The opponents may get in the bidding. In fact, they probably will, but they will be starting at an uncomfortable level. On this hand, 4♥ goes down one or two depending on whether the opponents can get a diamond ruff. In either case, they have a game and probably have a slam.

POSTMORTEM

I devised this rule a long time ago when I was trying to program a computer to bid. This was one of the few rules the computer could understand. It's a winner.

North Deals   +   No One Vulnerable

WEST

♠ 9 8 6 5 4 2
♥ 8
♦ K 6
♣ J 6 4 2

WEST	NORTH	EAST	SOUTH
	1♣	1♥	1NT
?			

SHOULD WEST BID 2♠ or should he pass?

WEST	NORTH	EAST	SOUTH
	1♣	1♥	1NT
Pass	Pass	2♥	Dbl
?			

West should not bid 2♠ over 1NT. The question was a little bit of a red herring. If the spades were headed by the QJ instead of the nine, I would be a bidder. Not, though, with the hand given.

East seems to have a good hand since he was willing to compete to 2♥ after South had announced a heart stopper and some values.

South doubles 2♥ for penalty.

For the second time in this auction West has a chance to bid 2♠. Would you think 2♥ doubled is the right contract, or is it time to mention spades?

WEST	NORTH	EAST	SOUTH
	1♣	1♥	1NT
Pass	Pass	2♥	Dbl
All pass			

West should pass. There are times to run and times to stay. Here, East was aware that South had something in hearts and East knew from the bidding that West rates to be weak. East bid 2♥ knowing full well that he might be doubled.

West has a king, which is potentially excellent. Believe me, East will be content with this dummy. It could be worse.

Here is the complete hand:

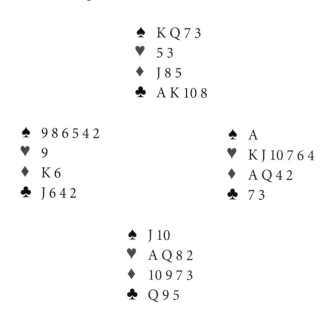

South led the ♠J. East took his ace and then took three diamond tricks and ruffed a diamond in dummy. He lost three heart tricks but it all added up to making 2♥ doubled.

If West had run to 2♠, he would have turned a great score into a terrible score. 2♠ looks to be down two against sensible defense, and it surely would be doubled.

The key is that East had to be serious about his heart suit when he bid it twice on a sequence where there was a known danger.

POSTMORTEM

Say the bidding had been different.

WEST	NORTH	EAST	SOUTH
	1♣	1♥	Pass
Pass	Dbl	Pass	Pass
?			

On this auction, East hasn't implied great hearts. He could have a normal overcall with five cards and a couple of honors. This sequence warns West that South has good hearts and his hand tells him that East is in trouble. Because East doesn't need the same great suit that he promised on the previous sequence, it is fine for West to bid 1♠.

West Deals   +   North-South Vulnerable

WEST	EAST
♠ J 10 9 8 6 5 2	♠ A K 4
♥ 4	♥ J 8 7 3
♦ 6 3	♦ K 10 7 5 2
♣ Q 7 3	♣ 9

WEST	NORTH	EAST	SOUTH
3♠	Dbl	4♠	5♥
All pass			

YOU MAY NOT feel this West hand measures up to a 3♠ preempt. If you don't like the bid, feel free to pass on such hands. It is a fact, though, which you will learn over time, that aggressive preempting is effective. The trick will be learning when to use bids like this.

For now, it is enough that this bid is presented as an example of something for you to think about in the future.

Note that East raises to 4♠ and then shuts up when South bids 5♥. Pushing the opponents up is usually an excellent result in itself and it is not necessary to double unless you are sure they are going down. The auction as given is good competitive bridge. I have preached for a long time about pushy preempts. As long as you peek at the vulnerability first, it is a winning tactic.

South Deals + North-South Vulnerable

	WEST		EAST
♠	A K J 7 3	♠	Q 10 9
♥	9 3	♥	10 6
♦	K 10 7	♦	Q 8 5 2
♣	J 4 2	♣	K 10 6 3

WEST	NORTH	EAST	SOUTH
			1♥
1♠	2♥	2♠	4♥
?			

WEST WAS FACED with a common bidding problem. He overcalled 1♠ and got a raise from his partner. When South bid 4♥, West had a decision. Let South play in 4♥ or bid 4♠, expecting to go down a trick or two. If South can make 4♥, that would be worth 620 points, so West only has to take seven tricks to show a profit.

Should West bid 4♠?

WEST	NORTH	EAST	SOUTH
			1♥
1♠	2♥	2♠	4♥
All pass			

West has a balanced hand and that is usually a signal that it is best to defend. There are some other reasons to pass, too.

The biggest is that 4♥ does not have to be making. Look at both hands. East and West have two potential spade winners. East and West have two potential diamond winners. And, East and West have two potential club winners. Your ♦10 and your partner's ♣10 turn out to be useful defensive cards. Either or both of them may turn into the setting trick.

It is not impossible that East and West will take four tricks on defense.

South may have bid 4♥ hoping that you would bid 4♠. This is a frequent strategy. South also could not have been sure that he would make 4♥ when he bid it. He may find his dummy with the wrong high-card points.

This last point is easy to prove. Have you ever bid a game and gone down? What happened was that you either bid too much or were unlucky. Why can't one of these things happen when your opponents bid to a game? Are they that much better bidders than you?

I doubt it.

Imperfection reigns in this game. Live with it.

POSTMORTEM

There is one more reason for passing 4♥ that is rather interesting and which is not very well known.

If your partner had bid 3♠ instead of two, how would you play that bid?

If you answer that the jump to 3♠ shows a weakish raise with four or more trumps, then you have a reasonable inference that your partner has three trumps.

No guarantees here but it's an inference you should not lose sight of.

If your partner has three spades and not four, that increases the odds on your side having two spade winners on defense. A good omen.

Bridge is full of little secrets. I'm hoping in this book, and in following books, to reveal many of them. I doubt you will find them anywhere else. If they were, they wouldn't be secrets.

North Deals   +   East-West Vulnerable

WEST

♠ J 10 7 6 4 3 2
♥ 8 6 5 3
♦ —
♣ 10 3

WEST	NORTH	EAST	SOUTH
	1♥	2♦	Pass
?			

THIS IS A recurring theme. Should West bid 2♠ or should he pass after East's overcall?

Which do you choose?

WEST	NORTH	EAST	SOUTH
	1♥	2♦	Pass
Pass	Dbl	Pass	Pass

West definitely should pass. 2♠ would not be forcing, at least in my opinion, but it does show invitational values. If your spades were headed by the the ace you would have a 2♠ bid. With the actual hand, passing is correct.

You get a second chance. North reopens with a double and South passes for penalty. Should you sit still or should you run to 2♠?

WEST	NORTH	EAST	SOUTH
	1♥	2♦	Pass
Pass	Dbl	Pass	Pass
2♠	Pass	Pass	2NT
Pass	3NT	All pass	

Running to 2♠ is correct. You have seven spades, not a motley five or six of them, and you have the worst possible number of trumps for your partner. Bidding 2♠ is a heartfelt effort to save your partner from disaster.

You will note that they found a way to 3NT. They will make it easily. South has three diamond stoppers and they have plenty of tricks.

If you had bid 2♠ immediately, your partner might have bid again. He has a good hand and from his point of view, your side might have 3NT. If your hand included the ♣A and a couple of diamonds, 3NT would have a play.

POSTMORTEM

Here's the layout:

```
              ♠  K Q 5
              ♥  A J 10 9 4
              ♦  9 3
              ♣  Q J 5

♠  J 10 7 6 4 3 2          ♠  8
♥  8 6 5 3                 ♥  K 2
♦  —                       ♦  A K J 7 6 2
♣  10 3                    ♣  K 7 6 2

              ♠  A 9
              ♥  Q 7
              ♦  Q 10 8 5 4
              ♣  A 9 8 4
```

West did well to pass and later run to 2♠. If you bid 2♠ earlier you will get too high and likely will be doubled.

Against 2♦ doubled, South will lead the ♥Q. East will lose one spade, one heart, three diamonds, and four clubs. Even if declarer can save a trick, 2♦ doubled is a bad result.

In 2♠ doubled, West will get four spades, one heart, and two diamonds. Even if doubled, that isn't bad. 3♠ doubled would have been bad.

The thing that West should take from this hand is that a 2♠ bid on the first round is invitational at least. Some pairs play 2♠ as forcing. Passing is an effort to keep from getting too high. Call it an avoidance play.

Learn it.

South Deals   +   East-West Vulnerable

	WEST		EAST
♠	A Q 4	♠	K
♥	A K	♥	Q 6 5 2
♦	K J 7 6 4 2	♦	Q 10 8 5
♣	A 9	♣	K J 7 6

WEST	NORTH	EAST	SOUTH
			3♠
3NT	All pass		

OVER SOUTH'S ANNOYING 3♠ bid, West has no good bid. Double risks partner bidding hearts with four of them. 4♦ isn't very enterprising and in any event, partner won't expect West to have this good a hand. 3NT is the only bid that rates to survive. It is the right bid, but it doesn't come with any promises. If East has a weak hand with a singleton or doubleton diamond, 3NT may go down three or four tricks.

East has to pass. Looking at the two hands, it looks silly to pass when 6NT is cold. But it is correct. The reason East should pass is that West's 3NT bid came under duress. West may have stretched with a sixteen- or seventeen-count, in which case East's eleven points will be enough to make 3NT with an overtrick.

This result is typical of what happens when a preemptor finds the opponents with good hands. There was no way for East to know that West had 21 points and there was no way for West to find out if East had anything without getting higher than 3NT.

POSTMORTEM

South made a lousy preempt and he got away with it.
Note that West would bid 3NT without the ♣A.

East Deals + North-South Vulnerable

	WEST		EAST
♠	8 7 3	♠	Q 10 4 2
♥	6 3	♥	K 9 8
♦	9 3 2	♦	A 5 4
♣	K Q J 10 8	♣	9 7 4

WEST	NORTH	EAST	SOUTH
		Pass	Pass
?			

AT FAVORABLE VULNERABILITY, there are two passes to you in third seat. In third seat, there is room for creative bidding. At this vulnerability, there is special motivation for creative bidding.

Can you think of anything to do here?

WEST	NORTH	EAST	SOUTH
		Pass	Pass
3♣	3♥	Pass	4♥
All pass			

I offer this hand as an example of something you can do in third seat. Passing is beyond criticism. But if you wish, there is a bid you might try. West's 3♣ bid looks odd, but it is really an OK bid. In third seat, you can and should open a weak two-bid with abandon. Five-card suits are fine in third seat. Regrettably your suit is clubs, else you would (should) open with a weak two-bid. Solution? Bid 3♣. And apologize if it doesn't work.

Notice that East was quiet throughout the auction. He correctly gave West room in the bidding. As a rule, you shouldn't raise partner's third-seat preempt unless you are sure it is right. The hand East has here has three-card support but it has boring values and shape.

On this hand nothing much happened, but there are some bright sides to the result. East led a club, something he might not have done had West never bid. And your opponents will see what West did, which will cause their hackles to go up next time they see him. If you can get your opponents to be suspicious of you, that is good.

East Deals + North-South Vulnerable

	WEST	EAST	
	♠ A Q 10 5 2	♠ K J 9 8	
	♥ 2	♥ A Q 8 5 3	
	♦ Q 7	♦ A 3	
	♣ A Q 7 6 4	♣ K 2	

WEST	NORTH	EAST	SOUTH
		1♥	Pass
1♠	Pass	3♠	Pass
?			

WEST HAS A sensational hand. How can he learn what he needs to know? For starters, 4NT is a bad choice. West is worried about diamonds. Better to explore first.

WEST	NORTH	EAST	SOUTH
		1♥	Pass
1♠	Pass	3♠	Pass
4♣	Pass	4♦	Pass
?			

East's cuebid solved the diamond problem. It would have been foolish to bid a slam missing two diamond tricks.

What now?

WEST	NORTH	EAST	SOUTH
		1♥	Pass
1♠	Pass	3♠	Pass
4♣	Pass	4♦	Pass
4NT	Pass	5♣	Pass
?			

West used keycard Blackwood and East showed three keycards. Since West has two aces, East is known to have the ♠K and the other two aces.

Does West know enough to make a final decision? How should West continue?

WEST	NORTH	EAST	SOUTH
		1♥	Pass
1♠	Pass	3♠	Pass
4♣	Pass	4♦	Pass
4NT	Pass	5♣	Pass
5NT	Pass	6♣	Pass
?			

This bid needs some explaining. When you are looking for a slam and have asked for aces, asking for kings with 5NT is not always the best treatment. The problem is that if more than one king is missing, it could be useful to learn which kings partner has, as opposed to how many kings East has. In this context, 6♣ shows the ♣K and it does not deny another king.

If East had no new kings to show (he has shown the king of trumps already) he would sign off in 6♠.

So West knows that East has the ♣K. Is this enough information to make a final bid?

Have you made up your mind yet?

WEST	NORTH	EAST	SOUTH
		1♥	Pass
1♠	Pass	3♠	Pass
4♣	Pass	4♦	Pass
4NT	Pass	5♣	Pass
5NT	Pass	6♣	Pass
7♠	All pass		

West knows that East has four spades and five or six hearts. No matter what East's distribution, West knows that all of East's minor-suit cards are covered. There are no minor-suit losers.

I think that West can risk bidding a grand here.

POSTMORTEM

Look at the two hands. How do you play in 7♠ when North leads the ♦10?

Assuming you take the ♦A, what card do you play from dummy next? Be specific.

Play the ♥A. Obviously, if spades and clubs divide nicely, you are cold for 7♠. The ♥A is a play that adds to your chances.

Here is West's plan:

1. Win the ♦A. No finesse at trick one.
2. Win the ♥A.
3. Ruff a heart in your hand with a high trump.
4. Go to dummy with a club.
5. Ruff a heart in your hand with a high trump. Assuming both defenders follow, you are cold.
6. Go to dummy with a trump.
7. Ruff another heart in your hand with a high trump. This sets up dummy's long heart.

8. Go to dummy with your last trump and draw any trumps that are still in play.
9. Claim. Dummy's heart is good and the three top clubs will take care of dummy's diamond.

This line is superior to others because it works even if clubs divide badly. In fact, you can make slam if clubs are bad and trumps are bad as long as hearts divide 4-3 or if the king falls. If after ruffing the third heart you see they are breaking badly, you can still fall back on other lines.

West Deals   +   North-South Vulnerable

WEST	EAST
♠ 9 8 3	♠ 6
♥ K Q 6 3	♥ J 10
♦ A 8 3	♦ 10 6 5 2
♣ A Q 10	♣ K 9 7 6 5 2

WEST	NORTH	EAST	SOUTH
1NT	Pass	?	

WEST OPENS A strong notrump which finds East with not much. Does your partnership have a way to sign off in 3♣? If so, do you want to do that?

WEST	NORTH	EAST	SOUTH
1NT	Pass	3♣	All pass

This is a simple approach and in the absence having four-way transfers to use, playing a jump to three of a minor as a signoff is pretty effective.

One big deal is that if you start with 2♣, South will be able to come in with 2♠. If you use 2♠ as a transfer to clubs, South will double. In either of these cases, North-South may be able to get into the bidding. They happen to have a little shape and can actually make 3♠.

The direct 3♣ bid may be enough to keep them out of the auction.

Note that 3♣ is defined as weak. There is not a shred of invitation to it.

If West had a maximum with a good club fit he may flirt with bidding again, but he does so on his own. East's hand is about what's expected. If West had the ♥AK instead of the ♥KQ, he might be entitled to dream about bidding 3NT. There could be nine tricks if the opening lead was a red card.

West Deals + No One Vulnerable

WEST	EAST
♠ A 6 2	♠ Q 8 4
♥ K J 7 6 2	♥ Q 8 3
♦ A 6 5 2	♦ K 10 9 8
♣ 3	♣ A 8 5

WEST	NORTH	EAST	SOUTH
1♥	Pass	3♥	Pass
4♥	All pass		

THIS IS THE bidding that occurred at the table. West opened 1♥ and East made a limit raise. West had only twelve points but he had aces and shape, so he went to game.

How good a game is this?

Basically, it makes if North has the ♠K and the trumps divide three-two. The ♠K will be onside half of the time and the trumps will divide three-two just under 70% of the time. This means game is about 35%. Yes, there are other considerations, such as something good happening in diamonds, but for the moment, let's forget about that.

Was this a good auction? Since the game was thin, might it be reasonable to suggest someone bid too much? Was it West? Was it East? Or was the bidding fine with you?

Your answer doesn't have to agree with mine, but I think the bidding was pretty awful. There's one bid that I abhor.

It was East's 3♥ bid. East made a limit raise with three hearts to the queen. This is one of the worst bids in bridge. When you make a limit raise, the first quality you have to have is four-card support. East violated this major rule.

Why is having four trumps such a big deal? West has five of them. That means your side has eight, and that is enough to be a good trump suit.

All true. The big problem is that West is expecting four and he will bid as if East has four. Take this hand. West went to game with his minimum. He did so because he expected there to be nine trumps which, as anyone knows, makes the play of the hand much easier than when there are just eight.

Let's make a change or two in the East hand:

♠	A 6 2	♠	10 8
♥	K J 7 6 2	♥	Q 8 4 3
♦	A 6 5 2	♦	K 10 9 8
♣	3	♣	A 8 5

In this layout, East has one more trump and no ♠Q. Game is still not cold but it is improved dramatically. You have one less spade loser to worry about and the chances of a second trump loser have dropped from 32% to under 10%.

♠	A 6 2	♠	8 4
♥	K J 7 6 2	♥	A 8 4 3
♦	A 6 5 2	♦	K J 9 7
♣	3	♣	9 8 5

In this layout East has eight high-card points but does have the promised four-card heart support. He has modest shape. Game is very good. If hearts are 2-2, it's almost cold. If hearts are 3-1, you might make 4♥ if diamonds are good for no losers. A good game to be in.

POSTMORTEM

It's important to let partner know how many trumps you have. If you have the East hand at the start of this article, you have many ways to show a limit raise with three-card support. Use one of them. Don't be lazy.

QUICKIE

Here's a curious fact. If you are missing four cards in a suit, they will divide 2-2 only 40% of the time. They will divide 3-1 around 50% of the time.

Say this is your trump suit.

♠ A 8 7 4   ♠ K J 5 3 2

All other things being equal, should you play the ace (both opponents playing a low spade) and then finesse for the queen, or should you play the ace and then the king, hoping for the queen to drop?

It's true that spades are more likely to divide 3-1 originally but the odds are now in favor of playing the king on the second round.

The reason is based on an interesting fact.

When you play the ace and the queen remains outstanding, you have learned that all of the 3-1 divisions that included a singleton queen are now tossed aside. Those cases are discarded.

At this point, there are more cases where the spade suit was originally 2-2 than cases where an opponent has Qxx facing a singleton. Good to know.

North Deals   +   North-South Vulnerable

WEST

♠ 3 2
♥ A J 10 9 7 6
♦ A J 4
♣ 3 2

WEST	NORTH	EAST	SOUTH
	1♣	Pass	1♥
?			

NORTH OPENED 1♣ and South bid 1♥, a suit you had hoped to bid yourself. Is there anything you can do other than pass?

There's a bidding trick that optimistic bidders may like. Bid 2♥.

This is not intended as a cuebid. It's a natural bid. When your RHO responds in a suit at the one level, it has turned out to be a very good idea to bid their suit when you have a fine suit of your own. They often respond with four rags in this suit. By bidding 2♥, you show these things:

1. A superb five-card suit or a good six-card suit. Be sure your suit has some spot cards in it. A86543 is not an acceptable suit.

2. You have a fair hand. Since you may get doubled, you need more than just a good suit. You need some other tricks too. 11–12 quality points in total is about right. This suit is good enough to upgrade a point or two.

Your opponents won't be pleased. The opening bidder may have wanted to bid 1♠. He can't. He may have been ready to rebid 2♣. He can't. He may be leery about bidding notrump. Your overcall will prove to be a very effective tool. But make sure you and partner are on the same wavelength.

South Deals + East-West Vulnerable

	WEST		EAST
♠	8 7 2	♠	K 5 3
♥	A K 10 7 3	♥	Q 8 4
♦	K 7 3	♦	J 10 4 2
♣	9 3	♣	A J 5

WEST	NORTH	EAST	SOUTH
			1♣
1♥	1♠	?	

EAST HAS A nice hand after West's overcall, but it does have some suspect values. How should East go about showing his hand after North's 1♠ bid?

WEST	NORTH	EAST	SOUTH
			1♣
1♥	1♠	2♣	Pass
2♥	3♣	?	

East's 2♣ cuebid almost always shows a good raise for partner. It is rare that East has anything other than a raise. West has fair values but overall, this is a minimum hand. He rebids 2♥. North competes with 3♣.

Do you think that the East hand has anything additional to say or did East do enough with the 2♣ bid?

WEST	NORTH	EAST	SOUTH
			1♣
1♥	1♠	2♣	Pass
2♥	3♣	Pass	Pass
?			

East does well to give up. His 2♣ bid said, approximately, that he had ten or eleven support points for hearts. That is exactly what he has. If anyone is to bid again, it will be up to West.

Should West bid again?

West should not. He expects that East has three hearts. Eight-card fits don't play as well as nine-card fits. West has a balanced hand. If West had better shape, he could consider bidding 3♥. If he had six cards in hearts he could consider bidding 3♥. All in all, this hand should be passed out in 3♣.

POSTMORTEM

How would 3♥ have fared?

It rates to lose two or three spades, perhaps a heart, two diamonds barring a miracle, and a sure club. 3♥ has a very slim chance of making.

How would 3♣ do?

South may or may not have a spade loser. South may have two heart losers. South certainly has a diamond loser and perhaps two. And South has problems in the club suit. Making 3♣ is slightly against the odds.

Some science: East has just three-card support. This is normal for hands that make a cuebid. If East had a limit raise with four hearts, he could make a jump cuebid of 3♣ showing, among other things, that he has a fourth trump.

If East makes a cuebid, implying three-card support, he can cuebid and later raise, but that would require at least thirteen decent points.

When you postmortem hands like this one, one of the things you have to consider is whether they would have made their contract. Looking at the East-West hands, you would expect 3♣ to be nip and tuck.

Final point: If you noted the vulnerability, you would be extra motivated to leave 3♣ alone. In 3♥, minus 100 is likely and minus 200 isn't far away. If someone doubled it, minus 500 would be possible. This can happen when both hands are balanced and finesses lose.

QUICKIE

A twelve-time world champion once found himself in 4♠ holding the following trump suit.

$$♠ \quad A \ Q \ 10 \ 5 \ 4$$

$$♠ \quad J \ 9 \ 8 \ 7 \ 6$$

The defense took the first three tricks. South ruffed in at trick four and led the ♠J. Assume no useful clues.

What is South's best play? South should finesse. Here's why.

South must consider these four layouts after he sees West's play.

♠ K 3 2	♠ –
♠ K 3	♠ 2
♠ K 2	♠ 3
♠ 3 2	♠ K

If West has one of the three holdings that include the king, finessing is right. If West has the 32 and East the singleton king, going up with the ace is right. An easy way to think about this is a that a singleton king in the East hand is clearly less likely than the other three holdings. This particular world champion was a slow learner. He repeated this exact bad play more than once.

North Deals   +   East-West Vulnerable

WEST	EAST
♠ 9 7 6 5	♠ A K
♥ 10 9 7 6	♥ Q J 8
♦ 8 7 3 2	♦ A 6 4
♣ 6	♣ K Q 7 5 3

WEST	NORTH	EAST	SOUTH
	1NT	?	

NORTH OPENS 1NT (15–17), finding East with a much better hand. What can East do?

East happened to be playing Hamilton. Using Hamilton, East can't double to show points. A double would show a one-suited hand, suit unknown.

East is stuck. What East did was pass, hoping for the best.

Everyone passed and East was quite disappointed to find his opponent making eight tricks.

After the hand, West said that it was lucky they were playing Hamilton because if East doubled for penalty, East-West would get a bad result as they had no place to play.

So East, upon pondering this statement, agreed that it was good that he could not double for penalty. But in the back of his mind, East thought of what could have been if West had had a few points.

South Deals   +   No One Vulnerable

WEST	EAST
♠ K	♠ Q 10 7 6 3
♥ J 8	♥ 10 9 6
♦ A J 7 6 3	♦ K 5 2
♣ K J 8 7 3	♣ Q 6

WEST	NORTH	EAST	SOUTH
			2♥
?			

SOUTH OPENS WITH a weak 2♥ bid. Do you think that West or East should bid? If yes, what bids do you suggest?

WEST	NORTH	EAST	SOUTH
			2♥
All pass			

Firstly, West has to pass. He has nothing but garbage. 2NT is not unusual here. It shows a strong 1NT hand. Even if West had a way to show both minors, he should not do so. That would be bad judgment. The West hand has so many losers that barring finding East with a good fit, bidding will get you a minus score. By far, the best thing to do is pass and leave any balancing bids to East.

East also should pass. His hand is just too weak.

3♦ looks playable for a second but if you think about it, the odds are that North has the ♦Q, and he may have length. That's not the least of declarer's worries. He has to set up the clubs; not easy. And, he has to contend with the defenders leading three rounds of hearts. And, the specter of a penalty double should convince West to pass.

My very serious advice is that you do not play 2NT as unusual after the opponents' weak two-bids.

North Deals + North-South Vulnerable

WEST	EAST
♠ 8	♠ A Q 7 3
♥ J 10 6 5 2	♥ Q 9 8
♦ Q 9 5 2	♦ 7
♣ 10 8 2	♣ K J 7 6 3

WEST	NORTH	EAST	SOUTH
	1♦	Dbl	Rdbl
?			

WHAT SHOULD WEST bid?

West uses a bidding strategy that you should know. It's impossible that West has a good hand on this auction, with everyone else showing good hands. He will never have enough to make strong bids. But he may have enough distributional values to make a descriptive bid. West should bid 2♥, saying he has a bad hand but he has five or six hearts and a little shape.

What West has is actually slightly better than average. West is hoping that this bid will inconvenience the opponents. It may, on a good day, give East enough information to bid some more.

WEST	NORTH	EAST	SOUTH
	1♦	Dbl	Rdbl
2♥	3♦	?	

Should East bid again?

WEST	NORTH	EAST	SOUTH
	1♦	Dbl	Rdbl
2♥	3♦	Pass	?

East should pass 3♦ and take whatever comes of it. East has only three hearts and he has a normal double. Bidding again would not be wise at all.

POSTMORTEM

This is one of the most useful bids I know. Sadly, there are still some who have not learned this tactic.

Keep West's hand in mind when your partner is the one who bids 2♥.

West Deals + North-South Vulnerable

	WEST		EAST
♠	A K Q 6 3	♠	8 2
♥	J 7 3	♥	Q 9 6 2
♦	J 2	♦	A K 10 6 4
♣	J 10 3	♣	Q 4

WEST	NORTH	EAST	SOUTH
1♠	Pass	1NT	Pass
2♣	Pass	2NT	All pass

THIS HAND IS presented as an example of Two Over One bidding.

West opens 1♠ with his good suit and outside garbage.

East has a hand that would bid 2♦ in many methods. That would be a fine bid. However, in Two Over One bidding, going to the two level in a new suit promises enough points for game. This East hand is close to that but falls short by a point or two.

What East does do is bid 1NT. This is a special bidding trick that holds the Two Over One methods together. Alvin Roth of New York did well to come up with this treatment. Without it, the Two Over One system would fail.

What 1NT does is to oblige opener to bid again. Most of the time East has a normal 1NT bid just like in other systems. However, East can have ten- or eleven-point hands and might even have more in special circumstances.

So it is back to West. He has to bid something. If he has a six-card major, he can rebid that. If he has a lower-ranking four-card suit, he can bid that. On this hand he doesn't have a good rebid so he has to bid a three-card suit. The rule that applies in this circumstance is that he rebids his lowest three-card suit.

Hence the odd-looking 2♣ bid.

East gets his second chance and bids 2NT, not 2♦. 2NT says he has about eleven points and suitable stoppers. West, on this hand, has a minimum and passes.

POSTMORTEM

If East had bid 2♦ on the first round, he would be showing a better hand.

If East had bid 2♦ on the second round, he would be showing a worse hand. He might, for example, rebid 2♦ with this hand:

♠ 2
♥ 10 8 6 4
♦ Q 10 9 6 5 3
♣ A 8

On this auction, 2♦ would be a weak call and opener can pass, and often does pass. Bidding 2♦ on the eleven-point hand above would result in a lot of missed games.

An aside: Using Two Over One methods, what should West rebid after 1NT with this hand?

♠ K J 8 7
♥ K J 7 6 4
♦ A 8
♣ J 8

This shape is not good for these methods. What West has to do is bid 2♣.

- He can't bid 2♥. That promises six cards.
- He can't bid 2♠. That's a reverse showing a big hand.
- He can't pass. 1NT is forcing.
- He can't bid 2NT. That shows 18–19 high-card points.

His only bid is 2♣. Surprisingly, this is not dangerous. If East passes, he probably has five clubs. If East bids 2♦ or 2♥ you should be reasonably happy.

Learn this bid and then when it comes up, you won't have to worry about what to do.

Note that if opener is in third or fourth seat, a 1NT response to 1♥ or 1♠ is not forcing. I'll discuss this further in a later book in this series.

East Deals + North-South Vulnerable

	WEST		EAST
♠	Q 10 7 6 4 3	♠	2
♥	J 3	♥	K Q 9 7
♦	J 9 8 6	♦	K Q
♣	2	♣	A J 9 8 7 4

WEST	NORTH	EAST	SOUTH
		1♣	Pass
1♠	Pass	2♣	All pass

EAST OPENS A normal 1♣. Should West respond or should he pass? I think there is a lot to be gained by bidding. If East rebids 1NT, West will bid 2♠. If East raises spades, admittedly unlikely, West will pass.

In this case, East rebids 2♣. West should pass. He should not bid 2♠. If East bids something stronger, such as 3♣, 2NT, or 2♥, West will wish he hadn't read this article. Against these bad things, there are two large plusses for bidding.

1. It makes it harder for the opponents to bid.
2. If East has spade support, you will get out of 1♣, which usually will go down, into a spade contract that will often make.

West Deals   +   No One Vulnerable

WEST

♠ A Q 8 3
♥ 9 3
♦ A 8
♣ K Q 7 6 3

WEST	NORTH	EAST	SOUTH
1♣	Pass	1♥	Pass
1♠	Pass	4♠	Pass
?			

WEST TAKES PART in a common sequence. West opens 1♣ and rebids 1♠. I can't imagine anyone not bidding 1♠ but recently I saw someone bid 2♣. Don't do that. East is looking for a major suit and he could easily have four spades too. If West doesn't bid 1♠, the suit rates to get lost.

The real question in this hand is, what should West bid over 4♠? Should he pass or should he look for a slam? It's not hard to envision hands that East can have that will make a slam.

Here are a couple:

♠ A Q 8 3	♠ K 10 9 4
♥ 9 3	♥ A J 7 6
♦ A 8	♦ 7 3
♣ K Q 7 6 3	♣ A 4 2

If both black suits divide three-two, you have twelve tricks in spades. Slam is just under 50%.

♠ A Q 8 3	♠ K 10 9 4
♥ 9 3	♥ A K 8 4
♦ A 8	♦ K 3 2
♣ K Q 7 6 3	♣ 8 4

If spades are three-two and if the hand does not run into any bad breaks, you might make a slam. Slam is decent but not great.

♠ A Q 8 3	♠ K 10 9 4
♥ 9 3	♥ Q J 7 6
♦ A 8	♦ Q J 2
♣ K Q 7 6 3	♣ A 2

No slam here.

♠ A Q 8 3	♠ K 10 9 4
♥ 9 3	♥ A K 10 6
♦ A 8	♦ Q J 4
♣ K Q 7 6 3	♣ 10 2

This might make a slam but it's way against the odds.

The point is that the West hand is good enough to ponder bidding further. If East has a minimum balanced raise to 4♠, slam is unlikely or impossible. If East has a good raise to 4♠, slam ranges from OK to very good.

Here is the reasoning West should use:

East had two ways to get to 4♠.

One. He could jump to 4♠, as he did. This bid shows game values with nothing exceptional.

Two. He could bid 2♦, the fourth-suit-forcing bid, and then bid 4♠. He would do that with this hand:

♠ A Q 8 3	♠ K J 9 4
♥ 9 3	♥ A Q 7 6
♦ A 8	♦ 10 9 3
♣ K Q 7 6 3	♣ A J

These two hands are a big favorite to produce a slam. Note that responder should not have more than an excellent fifteen points or a good sixteen points. With more, he has to be even more aggressive. West, expecting East to have a good raise to 4♠, courtesy of East's using fourth suit before bidding 4♠, is entitled to be optimistic.

POSTMORTEM

Many of my readers will remember Barry Crane. He was an incredible player. His typical routine was to fly across the country to play in the last two days of a regional. It was not uncommon for him to win both events.

For a few years Barry and I would play one or two events a year. I never matched up well with him and we usually had one bad game per day. He took it in good stride and I think he made our yearly game a personal obligation until we won an event. We did win some team games but never a pairs game.

One of the reasons we didn't do well was that I had a particularly annoying habit of envisioning hands for him. We would bid thus and such and I would start to think about what he might have. I would conclude that if he had certain cards we would make a slam, and I duly bid it.

He never had them.

After a few sessions of my bidding this way, Barry finally took me aside and told me in stern terms.

"Mike. If you ever need me to have specific cards to make a slam, don't bid it. I will never have them."

This piece of advice was among the best I ever got from anyone. The idea is that if you know your partner has exactly thirteen points, the odds on his having the thirteen points you want are slim.

Look for slam when you are sure about it or when you have room to find out.

On the West hand at the start of this article, I could flaunt the Barry Crane rule and bid higher, hoping for magic, or I could play in 4♠ and take a sure plus.

Having two ways for responder to show game values on this auction is very helpful. When opener knows he is facing a weak game hand versus a nice game hand, he will be better placed.

Let partner know this trick too.

East Deals + East-West Vulnerable

WEST	EAST
♠ Q 10 7 6 5 3	♠ 4
♥ K 10 8 5	♥ A 7
♦ 2	♦ A 10 7 6 3
♣ J 4	♣ K Q 9 8 3

WEST	NORTH	EAST	SOUTH
		1♦	Pass
1♠	Pass	2♣	Pass
2♠	Pass	?	

WEST BIDS AND rebids spades, which gives East a typical second round decision. Should he pass 2♠ or should he rebid clubs, hoping for a better fit?

WEST	NORTH	EAST	SOUTH
		1♦	Pass
1♠	Pass	2♣	Pass
2♠	All pass		

East ought to pass. West promises six spades, meaning that spades is an OK trump suit. If East bids again, he is making a wish that his partner has three cards in one of the minors. If West has only two cards in clubs or diamonds, being in three of that minor will not be an improvement.

Learning to give up in the face of a potential misfit is a good quality.

East should actually feel pretty good about playing in spades. He has three winners on top, which is not always the case.

The West hand has some pointers to offer. The first is the already-made observation that West needs six spades to make this bid. If he has five he should find another bid, if not a pass. I accept that some exceptions to this rule exist, but not very many.

Note that West did not bid 2♥. A 2♥ bid is forcing. Some partnerships might not play this particular fourth suit bid as forcing to game but it is forcing for one round. If you bid 2♥ and your partner rebids 2NT or 3♣, you will have made matters worse.

Here are a few hands that West might have after hearing partner open 1♦ and rebid 2♣.

> ♠ A Q 9 8 6 5 3
> ♥ 8 5
> ♦ 6 2
> ♣ Q 8

This is close to a maximum 2♠ bid. In this example West happens to have seven spades, one more than normal.

> ♠ J 10 8 6 3 2
> ♥ K 6 4
> ♦ 5 2
> ♣ Q 6

A lousy 2♠ bid. West really hopes to end the bidding here.

♠ A 8 7 6 3
♥ Q 9 8 7 4
♦ 9 4
♣ 5

Bid 2♦. Do not rebid 2♠, risking playing in a five-one fit, or 2♥, which is forcing and will push the bidding higher than you want.

On a few occasions, East will have four hearts and bidding 2♦ will get you to a horrible partscore, one that you will remember for awhile. Forget it. Bad things can happen.

♠ A K J 7 4
♥ Q 6 4
♦ J 3
♣ 9 7 2

Bid 2NT. Not forcing, but showing invitational values with hearts stopped. Your bid does not deny five spades.

♠ K Q J 7 4
♥ 9 7 2
♦ 8 3
♣ 10 5 4

It might be wise to pass 2♣. You will find that if your partner is rebidding correctly, he often has a singleton in your suit when he bids one of a suit and then two of a lower-ranking suit. This is a clear warning that bidding your suit again will leave you in a five-one fit.

♠ K 8 6 5 3
♥ 5 4
♦ 8 3
♣ A Q 5 3

Raise to 3♣. If your partner has three-card spade support, he may be able to show it next. Usually what happens is that your partner passes 3♣ or looks for 3NT. In either of these cases, your 3♣ bid will get you to a better contract than bidding 2♠.

♠ A Q J 7 4
♥ 8 7 4
♦ K 3
♣ Q J 3

Bid 2♥, the fourth-suit-forcing bid. This will get some kind of bid from your partner which should let you judge the right game contract. No number of spades is a good bid at this point.

2♠ is too weak a bid and it promises six spades.

3♠ is wrong for various reasons, one of them being that it promises six good spades.

2♥ lets you explore for notrump from your partner's side of the table and it also gives your partner a chance to show spade support if he has any.

	WEST	EAST
♠	A K J 3 2	9 4
♥	Q 3 2	K J 5
♦	7 3	A K J 9 4
♣	K 9 8	A Q J

WEST	NORTH	EAST	SOUTH
1♠	Pass	2♦	Pass
2NT	Pass	?	

EAST HAS A pretty nice hand. It's one of those hands that wants to look for a slam, but is in the shadow zone since it's difficult to show these values. You can just shoot out a slam but that does not have to be a winning approach.

What should East bid over 2NT? Is it acceptable to bid 6NT or should he try something else?

WEST	NORTH	EAST	SOUTH
1♠	Pass	2♦	Pass
2NT	Pass	4NT	All pass

East's best bid is 4NT. This is not Blackwood. It's an invitational bid. West is showing 12–14. 4NT asks if opener has a minimum or something better. You can see that 6NT might make but it would take a combination of good luck. Your nineteen points facing a thirteen-point hand doesn't rate to be worth twelve tricks.

A winning diamond or spade finesse isn't enough. If you take a finesse and it wins, you still need a lot more good luck. Slam is poor.

If East wished to ask for aces, he could use 4♣. A jump to 4♣ after a 1NT or 2NT bid from partner is Gerber. I'm not a fan of Gerber but when it is used properly, it holds its own. On this hand, 4♣ would be a mistake. East has only hopes that there are enough points. 4NT will find out what West thinks of his hand.

Many demerits for anyone who bids 4NT in response to 1♠. Never use Blackwood if you don't know where you're going.

West Deals + East-West Vulnerable

WEST

♠ 4 3
♥ A Q 9 8 3
♦ A 10 3
♣ K J 7

WEST	NORTH	EAST	SOUTH
1♥	2♠	3♥	4♠
?			

WEST OPENED 1♥ and North made a weak jump overcall of 2♠. The opponents' competition had the auction up to 4♠ before West could speak again.

Ought West to bid anything here? If so, what should it be?

WEST	NORTH	EAST	SOUTH
1♥	2♠	3♥	4♠
Dbl	All pass		

I like a double, although West has no clear knowledge of where the tricks will come from. East did bid 3♥, which showed modest values. On balance, the hand ought to belong to East-West.

Your side usually has about 21 high-card points. They rate to go down much of the time. It's worth doubling to stop these players from messing with your auctions.

If they make it, I don't expect to get many matchpoints. However, if they go down, especially if they go down two, doubling is good because it puts us in contention for 300, a useful score if we can't make a game.

Here's the layout:

WEST	EAST
♠ 4 3	♠ 9 6
♥ A Q 9 8 3	♥ K 4 2
♦ A 10 3	♦ Q J 8 5 2
♣ K J 7	♣ Q 5 2

Looking at both hands, it's clear that we might make 4♥. If West bids 5♥, he will go down. If West doubles, he rates to set 4♠ one or two or even three tricks. This is the best West can do under the circumstances.

Remember these doubles. When you have the majority of the points and they are at the four level, consider a double. This is especially true when you have a balanced hand.

North Deals   +   East-West Vulnerable

WEST

♠ 9 7 6 3
♥ A 2
♦ Q 6
♣ A J 9 8 7

WEST	NORTH	EAST	SOUTH
	3♠	5♦	Pass
?			

NORTH STARTS WITH 3♠ and East, vulnerable, bids 5♦.
What should you do with the West cards?

WEST	NORTH	EAST	SOUTH
	3♠	5♦	Pass
6♦	All pass		

You should bid 6♦. If you pass, thinking that there might be
two spade losers or that something bad might happen such as a
bad break in trumps, you are being pessimistic.

East just bid 5♦. He jumped to game. If he can bid 5♦ and
you can produce two aces and the ♦Q, you must have a play for
twelve tricks.

5♦ is not a weak bid. East would be foolish to preempt on top
of North's preempt. If East had a weak hand, the way he would
show it is by passing, not by jumping to 5♦.

Here's the layout:

WEST	EAST
♠ 9 7 6 3	♠ 10
♥ A 2	♥ 10
♦ Q 6	♦ A K J 10 9 5 4 3
♣ A J 9 8 7	♣ K Q 10

East's 5♦ bid was practical. West's raise was sane. West had three immensely important high cards. A very fair gamble.

RULE OF SEVEN

If you are familiar with the Rule of Seven, you will have another comparison to make. When your partner makes a bid over a preempt, he is always making a wish of sorts. He is wishing that you have something. About seven points is the traditional guideline of what he is allowed to wish for.

He bid 5♦, suggesting he is playing you for seven points. You have a super eleven points, more than he is expecting.

POSTMORTEM

Think about this hand in one last way. You have eleven nice points. Compare this hand with the following hand.

$$♠ \quad 9 7 6 3$$
$$♥ \quad Q J 9 2$$
$$♦ \quad 6$$
$$♣ \quad 7 6 5 3$$

This is a bad hand. Your partner won't love you for it but remember that he knew this was a possible hand. Since you have so much more than you might have had, it is very reasonable to bid one more.

Note the East hand. East did a good thing when he bid 5♦. 4♦ would be conservative. From East's point of view, 5♦ might make if West had a couple of little diamonds and the ♣A. East didn't wish to bid 4♦ only and have his partner pass on hands which would make 5♦ a good contract.

♠ 10
♥ 10
♦ A K Q 10 9 5 4 3
♣ A K Q

If you wait for a hand like this one to bid 5♦ over 3♠, you will miss out on many hands where you have a good hand that needs only a little help from partner. You have to assume your partner will have 'something' for you. Seven points from partner is a reasonable wish to make. Note, by the way, that even this hand can't guarantee making 5♦. If a defender has ♦Jxxx, you have three potential losers.

South Deals　+　East-West Vulnerable

WEST	EAST
♠ A K 9	♠ 8
♥ Q	♥ J 9 8 7 6 5 2
♦ A Q 2	♦ K 10 7 3
♣ A 9 8 7 6 2	♣ 5

WEST	NORTH	EAST	SOUTH
			3♠
3NT	Pass	?	

SOUTH OPENS 3♠ and West bids 3NT. This auction is terrible for East to respond to because West can have anywhere from a balanced fifteen-point hand up to a huge hand with a long suit and perhaps a singleton somewhere. It's possible that 3NT is the best spot.

East has to make an intelligent guess.

Here, with a 7-4 shape, bidding 4♥ makes good sense.

There is a little question of how to do that. If East-West are using transfer bids, he has to bid 4♦. If East-West are not using transfer bids, he has to bid 4♥. Do you know what your bids mean after partner's 3NT bid? Not many players do.

Should West be happy or unhappy with this?

West should be relatively happy. He did not promise any heart support and he does have a lot of aces and a king, good cards for a heart contract.

If West gets cold feet, he will run to 5♣ and that will be a disaster. 4♥ is the last making game contract for East-West.

HAND 62

	WEST	EAST
♠	Q J 7	♠ 9 2
♥	A J 8 3	♥ K 9 2
♦	K 2	♦ Q J 10 7 3
♣	A J 9 8	♣ K 7 4

WEST	NORTH	EAST	SOUTH
1NT	Pass	?	

WEST OPENS A strong notrump showing fifteen to seventeen points. What do you bid with the East hand?

WEST	NORTH	EAST	SOUTH
1NT	Pass	3NT	All pass

I root for 3NT. If West has fifteen points, you might have less than the classic requirement of 26 points, but that is a small issue.

East has nine points which are bolstered by a five-card suit and good spot cards, most notably the ♦10.

Bridge players today play better than they did thirty years ago and they properly bid to game on fewer values than they did then.

Here, 3NT makes unless spades divide five-three and they lead them. If South is the one with long spades, North won't know to lead them and West will have time to make nine tricks. West will also make nine tricks when spades are four-four.

If East didn't have the ♦10 bidding just 2NT would be OK, although I would still bid 3NT.

WEST	EAST
♠ Q J 7	♠ 9 2
♥ A J 8 3	♥ K 9 2
♦ K 2	♦ Q J 7 5 3
♣ A J 9 8	♣ K 7 4

Note how valuable the ♦10 is. With the ten, 3NT is good. Without it, 3NT is marginal.

HAND
63

WEST

♠ 8 7 3
♥ K J 6 2
♦ A J 5 4 3
♣ K

WEST	NORTH	EAST	SOUTH
1♦	1♠	3♠	4♠
?			

EAST'S 3♠ BID is a splinter bid. It shows game-forcing values with a diamond fit and a singleton spade. Splinters are useful tools, ranking up there near the top of my top ten list.

What should you bid with the West hand over 4♠?

WEST	NORTH	EAST	SOUTH
1♦	1♠	3♠	4♠
5♦	All pass		

West has an easy 5♦ bid. In fact, it's possible to make a case for bidding more than that. The big deal here is that West knows what kind of hand East has.

Here's the layout:

WEST		EAST	
♠ 8 7 3		♠ 10	
♥ K J 6 2		♥ A 7 5	
♦ A J 5 4 3		♦ K 9 7 6 2	
♣ K		♣ A J 7 4	

5♦ ends the auction and as you can see, slam is not terrible. Diamonds rate to break so slam depends on the heart finesse or perhaps an extra chance coming in.

If you ruff a club in your hand, the queen may come down, giving you a second heart discard. This is a slam that no one would mind bidding.

POSTMORTEM

East's splinter bid is the key here. In one bid it describes his shape and values. This is a good example of a minimum opening bid becoming better during the bidding. East-West have only 24 high-card points yet slam is reasonable.

Many players bid 2♠ with the East hand.

Some of them play 2♠ shows a limit raise or better.

Some of them play 2♠ shows a balanced game-forcing raise.

No matter how you play 2♠, it's a bad bid because it does not tell West the important news that East has a singleton spade. Imagine bidding the West hand if East had made a cuebid instead of a splinter bid.

West would worry about two spade losers and might not bid to game, let alone a slam.

The splinter bid does it all. It tells West of his shape, his values, his support, and it does so right away so West can judge what to bid over 4♠.

Solid Deals   +   North-South Vulnerable

WEST

- ♠ K 10 8 7 4
- ♥ K 3
- ♦ 9
- ♣ A 10 6 5 3

WEST	NORTH	EAST	SOUTH
			1♣
1♠	Pass	3♣	Pass
?			

WEST HAS AN easy overcall of 1♠. What should he do next after East's 3♣ bid?

WEST	NORTH	EAST	SOUTH
			1♣
1♠	Pass	3♣	Pass
4♠	All pass		

West should bid 4♠. The reason for bidding 4♠ is, of course, a function of what 3♣ meant. I know that not all players are familiar with this. It's a bit scientific, but it is an excellent tool to have.

3♣ is a jump in opener's suit. It is defined as showing a limit raise or better with four or more trumps. I have harped endlessly about not making jump raises without four-card support. This is just one more situation where that advice applies.

West has a modest trump suit but knowing of four-card support makes his hand a lot more attractive than it would be if East promised only three trumps. Here are the hands:

WEST	EAST
♠ K 10 8 7 4	♠ Q J 9 2
♥ K 3	♥ A 10 8 7
♦ 9	♦ K 10 3
♣ A 10 6 5 3	♣ J 8

East happens to have the ♣J but even without it, 4♠ is a decent contract. East also has the ♦K. It's not going to be worth much here.

POSTMORTEM

West had to judge just how good his hand is. This is an exercise in hand evaluation, one of the final hurdles for new players to overcome on their way to becoming good players.

Note that if East had one less spade, his proper bid would be 2♣. This cuebid usually shows support for the overcall along with limit raise values. The difference is that a 2♣ cuebid denies four trumps. A huge difference.

Every book extols the value of having an eight-card fit. Some call it the Golden Fit. It is logical that having a nine-card fit is better. Well, it is. If you have an eight-card fit, you will often come to grief when the trump suit divides 4-1. I bet you can remember this happening. It will never happen when you have nine trumps. I don't know the name for it. But I do know I like it.

WEST	EAST
♠ 3	♠ A 10 9 7
♥ K Q 10 8 6 5 3	♥ 2
♦ K 7 3	♦ A J 10 8
♣ 5 3	♣ K J 9 4

WEST	NORTH	EAST	SOUTH
3♥	Dbl	Pass	3♠
Pass	Pass	?	

WEST OPENED 3♥, which North doubled for takeout. East correctly passed and South bid 3♠. This got around to East. Should he do anything?

WEST	NORTH	EAST	SOUTH
3♥	Dbl	Pass	3♠
Pass	Pass	Dbl	All pass

Double gets my vote. East has potential tricks mixed with sure tricks. West, while not promising much, does promise whatever your partnership requires for a vulnerable 3♥ pre-empt. East appreciates his hand because his strength is behind the takeout doubler.

Here is the complete hand as seen by the unfortunate South player.

```
              ♠ K Q 5
              ♥ A 7
              ♦ Q 9 6 2
              ♣ A Q 10 2

  ♠ 3                          ♠ A 10 9 7
  ♥ K Q 10 8 6 5 3            ♥ 2
  ♦ K 7 3                      ♦ A J 10 8
  ♣ 5 3                        ♣ K J 9 4

              ♠ J 8 6 4 2
              ♥ J 9 4
              ♦ 5 4
              ♣ 8 7 6
```

South has two spade losers, a heart loser and another heart to worry about, two diamond losers, and two club losers. This is going to be an uphill battle for South.

Sometimes a player makes a normal bid and pays a price for it. Take this hand, for instance. North made a sane double but South has a lousy hand and doesn't have a good place to play. This happens.

POSTMORTEM

South might have passed 3♥ doubled for penalty instead of bidding 3♠, but that result is no better as West will make at least nine tricks and might make eleven.

It behooves you to be able to take advantage when your side's preempt catches the opponents.

1. South has five spades. Imagine how poor 3♠ doubled would be if South had just four of them.
2. If North didn't double 3♥ (on a different layout) East might have bid 4♥. However, if North passed, 4♥ would not be as good a contract since West wouldn't know where the high cards were.

QUICKIE

This is a reminder about an overlooked bid. Your partner opens 1♥. What is the right response with this hand?

♠ A J 8 3 2
♥ Q 8 3
♦ 8 6 5 4
♣ 6

Bid 2♥. You have what is called a 'one bid' hand. If you bid 1♠ and partner bids 2♣ or 2♦, you will have to bid 2♥ next. The trouble with this bid is that your partner won't know you really like hearts. He will fear that you are giving a preference to 2♥, which you would often do with only two hearts. Your best bid is to raise to 2♥ immediately, which tells partner precisely that you have heart support with about 6–9 points. This is an important hand to remember.

West Deals   +   East-West Vulnerable

WEST	EAST
♠ Q 10 9 7 5	♠ K J 2
♥ A 2	♥ 10 8 7 5 3
♦ A Q 8	♦ 2
♣ J 10 5	♣ K 6 4 2

WEST	NORTH	EAST	SOUTH
1♠	2♣*	3♠	All pass

*HEARTS AND A MINOR

IF YOU HAVEN'T run into these cuebids, you will soon enough. When you hear a cuebid, you should always find out what it is. In this case, it shows hearts and a minor suit. This is a form of the Michaels cuebid.

What should East do over 2♠? Should he double to show points? Should he pass? Is it right to bid 3♠ with only seven points and some shape?

The answer is that East should raise. In competition, you can raise to the three level with hands like this when you have been pushed into it. It would be wrong to double. Double says you have ten points and a hand that doesn't have a better bid available.

West has a normal opening bid so he passes. Note that the opponents have a diamond fit. They may be able to make 2♦ up to 4♦. East's raise makes it harder for them to find their diamond fit.

South Deals + No One Vulnerable

WEST	EAST
♠ A J 8 7 3	♠ Q 9
♥ K 4 2	♥ A J 8 7
♦ Q 9 8	♦ K J 3 2
♣ 8 2	♣ J 10 6

WEST	NORTH	EAST	SOUTH
			1♣
1♠	Dbl	?	

A USEFUL BIDDING trick.

Here is a problem that you have run into more than once. You are East. Your partner overcalls at the one level and the next player makes a negative double. What can you bid when you have a good hand with two-card support for your partner?

If you had three-card spade support you would bid 2♣, a cuebid, and then raise spades. Unfortunately, you have only two spades so you can't bid that way.

Is there a sensible bid you can make now or might it be better to pass and see how the bidding develops?

WEST	NORTH	EAST	SOUTH
			1♣
1♠	Dbl	Rdbl	2♣
Pass	Pass	2♠	All pass

There is a way to show this hand. Redouble. Your partner will know you have about eleven points or more and he will know you don't have three-card support. If you had three-card support, you would cuebid. A redouble denies three-card support. This is a very important distinction to make because when you redouble and then bid again, your partner knows something important about your distribution.

On this hand, South rebids his clubs and when this is passed to you, you are able to bid 2♠ without misdescribing your hand. West will understand that you have a nice hand with only two spades and he will know you don't have better than twelve points because you would try to find a different bid at this point.

POSTMORTEM

If West wishes to, he can double 2♣. He would do that if he had something in clubs.

♠ K Q J 9 3
♥ A 3
♦ 8 7
♣ Q 10 7 3

This would be a fine double of 2♣ if given the opportunity. West has a solid overcall and he knows East has eleven points. South is in trouble.

On the hand that West actually has, he would double 2♦ if South bid that.

East's redouble did a couple of things.

1. It gave East-West a chance to double something.
2. It gave East a way to raise spades without giving West the wrong impression about his spade support.

Imagine what East should bid if the redouble wasn't available.

WEST		EAST	
♠ 3 2		♠ K 8 6	
♥ K Q 7 6 3		♥ 10 5 2	
♦ K 8 7		♦ A J 9	
♣ J 4 2		♣ Q 8 7 3	

WEST	NORTH	EAST	SOUTH
	1♣	Pass	Pass
?			

West is in the balancing seat against North's 1♣ bid. He has a fair heart suit and enough values that he might have overcalled 1♥. Is it worth a 1♥ balancing bid?

WEST	NORTH	EAST	SOUTH
	1♣	Pass	Pass
1♥	1♠	2♥	2♠
All pass			

It's a close decision. On this hand, West did bid 1♥ and the bidding continued as shown. Opener rebid 1♠ and South, the hand that could not respond to 1♣, had enough spades that he could compete to 2♠.

This was a big swing because 1♣ was not a good contract for North. 2♠, on the other hand, was an excellent contract.

POSTMORTEM

How should West know what to do here? In my book *Balancing in Contract Bridge*, there are a number of concepts specifically aimed at reopening decisions. The one that applies here is the concept of 'missing majors'.

West should be worried about spades. It's not an overwhelming worry, but it is a real worry. East seems to have ten or more points and he did not overcall. This suggests he doesn't have five spades. If he has four, West doesn't have to worry too much about spades but if East has three or two, spades are a problem.

With close balancing decisions, the warning of missing suits should be heeded.

So how did you do? Did you defend 1♣ or 2♠?

West Deals + Both Sides Vulnerable

WEST	EAST
♠ A J 7 3	♠ 9 5
♥ 2	♥ J 7 3
♦ Q 10 8 3	♦ K 9 4
♣ K Q 6 2	♣ A 8 7 5 3

WEST	NORTH	EAST	SOUTH
1♣	Pass	2♣	Pass
?			

LET'S ASSUME YOU open 1♣. Some would bid 1♦ but in the long run, no one can say for sure which is best.

After your opening bid, East raises to 2♣. Would it occur to you to bid something or is passing best?

WEST	NORTH	EAST	SOUTH
1♣	Pass	2♣	Pass
3♣	All pass		

The reason for bidding 3♣ is simple. First of all, let me note that when your minor suit is raised, bidding three of the minor is competitive. This means that 3♣ by you is not invitational when the opponents are quiet or when they compete.

You can bet that your opponents aren't going to let you play in 2♣. This is a lock. Your singleton heart tells you that they have at least nine hearts and they also have half of the high-card points. It's likely that they can make 2♥ and three is definitely possible.

What you want to do is keep them out of the bidding. I like a 3♣ bid just for this reason. It may steal the pot.

The idea of good bidding is to find a fit and then decide how high to go. You have four clubs and your partner raised. He will almost always have four clubs and often five, and he also denies a major suit.

This means that you have a good fit and so do the opponents.

Having found a good fit you now have to decide how high to go. Since their side is likely to bid hearts, you are going to consider bidding 3♣ later. Better is to bid is now before they find their fit.

Note East's good 2♣ bid. Without this bid, this discussion would be academic. East was not excited about bidding notrump. He would prefer that West do that. Hence, the 2♣ bid. It identifies a fit and it also lets West know that if he wants to bid higher, he knows what East has.

> Finally, a reminder that one-two-three
> of a major suit is different.

If the opponents are quiet:

I suggest you play that in lieu of competition, you play this sequence as invitational. It asks for general strength.

WEST	NORTH	EAST	SOUTH
1♥	Pass	2♥	Pass
3♥			

If the opponents compete:

WEST	NORTH	EAST	SOUTH
1♥	Pass	2♥	2♠
3♥			

If they compete and bid over your partner's raise, a bid of three of your major is competitive, not invitational.

In the minors, a bid of three of that minor by opener is always competitive.

In the majors, opener's bid of three of the major is competitive only when opener's RHO has bid something.

QUICKIE

This one of my most useful hints. The opponents bid thusly.

WEST	NORTH	EAST	SOUTH
		1NT	Pass
2♣	Pass	2♥	Pass
3NT	All pass		

You are South. What do you lead? Here's a hint you can use to good effect. When your LHO bids Stayman and RHO shows a major and your LHO goes to 3NT, you know the following.

West has a four-card major. In this case, he has four spades.

East has a four-card major. In this case, he has four hearts.

Your partner did not double 2♣.

You should consider leading a diamond. It's not automatic, but it's a good thing to think about if you aren't sure what else to lead.

West Deals + East-West Vulnerable

	WEST		EAST
♠	7	♠	10 9 6
♥	A Q 7 4 2	♥	K
♦	K J 2	♦	Q 5 4 3
♣	Q 10 6 3	♣	K J 9 7 5

WEST	NORTH	EAST	SOUTH
1♥	Pass	1NT	Pass
2♣	Pass	2♠	Pass
3♣	All pass		

WEST OPENS 1♥ and East is obliged to bid 1NT. There is no other sane bid he can make. West rebids 2♣, which might be a three-card suit. Heck. It might be a doubleton.

East now has a hand that is way bigger than it was a moment ago. Finding a fit does that to a hand. East wants to raise clubs but how high should he go?

East bids 2♠. This is a useful convention called the impossible 2♠ bid. It works this way. When West opens specifically with 1♥ and East responds 1NT, opener often rebids 2♣ or 2♦. If East has an 8–9 point hand with a fit, he can raise the minor if it looks like the best bid. If responder has an even better hand with a fit, he bids 2♠ to show how happy he is with opener's minor.

West, on hearing the 2♠ bid (it is an alert), knows that clubs are going to be trumps. Since opener has a minimum hand, he just bids 3♣. East has a nice 2♠ bid but he has nothing extra so he passes 3♣.

The partnership, having learned a lot, plays in 3♣.

West Deals + North-South Vulnerable

	WEST		EAST
♠	8 7 5	♠	10 4
♥	A Q 10 7 6 5	♥	K 8 3
♦	A 10 5 3	♦	9 8 7 4
♣	—	♣	J 10 6 4

WEST	NORTH	EAST	SOUTH
1♥	Dbl	2♥	2♠
4♥	4♠	All pass	

THERE ARE LOTS of little points in this hand, and a couple
of big ones. Taking them in order, West opens 1♥ with only ten
high-card points. You can open ten-point hands when you have
all of the following:

1. You have aces and kings as opposed to a king and lots of
   queens and jacks.
2. You have very good shape.
3. You can rebid comfortably no matter how the auction
   goes.
4. You have two defensive tricks.

West has all four of these qualities so is entitled to open.

East's raise to 2♥ is a proven winning effort. The bidding is
going to be competitive so it is necessary for East to get his two
cents in right away. If East passes, he won't get a second chance.
Why should East bid with this piece of cheese? East should bid
so his partner, who has the big hand in the partnership, will be
able to continue if proper.

As long as East can count on West to remember that East's raise may be weaker than normal, East can make this raise without concern.

West bids 4♥ based on his six-card suit and his shape. If you choose to bid only 3♥ or to pass, I think that's too conservative. Winning bridge is consistent pushy bidding, not consistent thoughtful passing. Note I said 'pushy' bidding, not ludicrous bidding.

East, of course, passes 4♠ and it gets back to West to make the final decision. If West thinks 4♠ will make, he can bid 5♥ and hope to go down less than the value of 4♠. If West thinks 4♠ will go down, he should pass and try to beat it. What would you do?

You should pass. You have two aces and your partner has shown a few points.

PORTMORTEM

West's void in clubs is a suggestion that the opponents' side suit is breaking badly for them. If East has ♣Q1085, it might be a huge problem for North-South.

One important thought. East might have bid 3♥ if he had four hearts. It's likely that East has three hearts. It's not impossible that your side has two heart tricks.

South Deals + No One Vulnerable

	WEST		EAST
♠	Q 9 3	♠	A 10 6 2
♥	K 8 3	♥	4
♦	A 7 3	♦	K J 8 2
♣	Q J 3 2	♣	A 9 8 7

WEST	NORTH	EAST	SOUTH
			4♥
Pass	Pass	?	

THIS IS A judgment hand; nothing else. Judgment is that quality that learns from experiences, good ones and bad ones, helping you to recognize situations for what they are. Your judgment can also be improved by reading books that show decisions being made. Combining reading and experiences is important. What this means is that when you get a good or a bad result, you don't blame your partner when it's bad and you don't gloat when it's good. Instead, you study what happened. Perhaps you can get some advice from a good player. Always think and then later remember what the winning consideration(s) was last time.

On this auction, South opens 4♥ and East, in the reopening seat, has to decide whether to compete or pass.

What do you think East should do?

WEST	NORTH	EAST	SOUTH
			4♥
Pass	Pass	Dbl	All pass

East should make a takeout double, something he would not do in the immediate seat. In the reopening seat, it is acceptable to double with less than normal values. If you had the ♣K too, your hand would have enough to double 4♥ in either seat.

POSTMORTEM

East's double is not a stretch. It is a balancing bid. You can't be sure but it's very reasonable to expect partner to have some values. South's bid is preemptive and that means there are a lot of points in your partner's hand and in the dummy on your right. Most of the time your partner has half of those missing points.

Note that if the opening bid had been 4♠ and East had the same values with a singleton spade, bidding would be more dangerous because West would have to go to the five level if he chose to bid a suit. Over 4♥, there is the live possibility that West will bid spades, something he can do at the four level.

Note that West passed. He didn't bid 5♣. West has a balanced hand, which is a bad omen. He also has some points including the ♥K, a sure defensive trick but a trick that might not be helpful in a suit contract. West correctly decides to take a profit (hopefully) by defending instead of playing.

73

EAST

♠ Q J 9 6 5 2
♥ 9 2
♦ 8 4
♣ J 8 3

WEST	NORTH	EAST	SOUTH
1♦	Pass	?	

WEST OPENS 1♦, passed by North. What should East do?

A common treatment in use these days is the weak jump shift. If East-West are using this treatment, East can bid 2♠. This is quite different from using 2♠ to show a powerhouse hand with good spades.

2♠ is an example of a weak jump shift. Many forget this in the heat of battle. I'll assume that anyone reading this discussion will remember what it means.

The ranges that I suggest are as follows:

If not vulnerable, you can jump shift with a good two points up to five or so.

If vulnerable, you can jump shift with a fair three points up to a motley six points.

It's a good idea to have agreements, and that you follow them. Some players feel that a weak jump shift can be made on zero points. That's not my style. I don't like bidding with nothing because my partner will have hopes that I have a few points and may bid on that assumption.

Note that all weak jump shifts are at the two level. Higher jump shifts have different meanings.

Here's what a weak jump shift gains for you:

By bidding 2♠, you hinder their bidding and you calm your partner's nerves by telling him exactly what you have. If you bid 1♠, your partner won't know you are this weak. He will expect, or at least hope, that you have a better hand. If he starts making strong bids, you won't like it. Your 2♠ bid is so accurate that your side won't get higher unless it is right to do so. If your partner likes spades, he may be able to push the opponents higher.

Here's what a weak jump shift can cost you:

If you play weak jump shifts, you won't be able to make strong jump shifts any more. That's not actually a bad thing. Players today bid much better than they did years ago. Since a weak jump shift comes up twenty times as often as a strong jump shift, that's a good reason for using them. Another downside is that you may miss a better fit. Or you may have a misfit and get caught by a penalty double. That's been known to happen.

WEST	NORTH	EAST	SOUTH
1♣	Pass	?	

♠ 7 4
♥ Q 10 9 8 7 3
♦ 8 6 4 3
♣ 2

Bid 2♥, a sane minimum jump shift. Your suit is adequate, and that's a good start. Your shape is nice too.

♠ K J 8 7 6 4
♥ J 5 3
♦ 4 3
♣ 6 3

Bid 2♠. A fair maximum weak jump shift. 2♠ may work. It may not. In the long run, you will gain in many ways.

WEST	NORTH	EAST	SOUTH
1♦	Pass	?	

If you are vulnerable:

    ♠ 10
    ♥ Q J 10 7 6 3
    ♦ 4 3
    ♣ 9 5 4 2

Bid 2♥, a fine minimum. You don't have much but your suit is excellent. If you bid 1♥, you may be faced with a bid you don't like such as 2NT or 3♦ from your partner. If you pass 1♦, it's not likely to be a good contract.

    ♠ K Q 8 6 5 4
    ♥ 4 3
    ♦ 7 6 5
    ♣ 4 2

Bid 2♠. A maximum vulnerable weak jump shift. This hand has five decent points. With a good six, bid 1♠.

    ♠ A J 10 9 7 3
    ♥ 3
    ♦ 8 7 4 3
    ♣ 5 4

Bid 1♠. This hand has five high-card points, but it's better than the previous hand. The suit is superb. It's rare that you will make a weak jump shift with an ace in your hand.

How does opener bid when partner makes a weak jump shift? For starters, opener passes with most of his minimum hands.

If he has a fit and a normal opener, he can raise. A raise is not invitational. It is an effort to keep the opponents from bidding.

If opener rebids his original suit, it is a signoff bid.

If opener bids a new suit, it is forcing. Opener will seldom have a good enough hand for this bid.

If opener has a big hand with two-card support or more, and wants to invite game in partner's suit, he can bid 2NT, which asks partner to describe his hand. This is called Ogust, something that many people already use when responding to a weak two-bid.

WEST	NORTH	EAST	SOUTH
1♦	Pass	2♥	Pass
2NT	Pass	?	

3♣   I have as weak a hand as possible and I have a bad suit.

3♦   I have as weak a hand as possible but I have a decent suit.

3♥   I have a good hand (relatively speaking) but my suit is bad.

3♠   I have a good hand (relatively speaking) and I have a good suit.

Since everything is relative to your partnership style, I will leave it to you to decide which hands are good and which are bad. I remind you that if you agree to bid 2♥ or 2♠ on two to five points when not vulnerable, a four-point hand becomes a 'good' hand.

My idea of a good suit is also relative. You have to consider the spot cards as well as the high cards in the suit.

North Deals   +   North-South Vulnerable

WEST	EAST
♠ Q J 7 6 3	♠ K 8 4 2
♥ 5 3	♥ 9 8
♦ 4 2	♦ A Q 9 3
♣ 10 7 6 5	♣ K J 4

WEST	NORTH	EAST	SOUTH
	1♥	Dbl	2NT*
?			

*LIMIT RAISE

NORTH OPENS 1♥ and East doubles. South bids 2NT, the Jordan 2NT bid, showing a limit raise or better with four or more trumps.

Does West have a bid? West expects that North-South can make 4♥. Since they are vulnerable and you are not, there could to be a good save in 4♠. West should bid 3♠. He might even bid 4♠.

If North-South can make 4♥, it is worth 620 points. There is an excellent chance that West will get out for -300 or -500.

Note that if North bids 4♥ over 3♠, likely, East can bid 4♠ or pass. He has some defense and he knows leading a spade has potential.

If East had a singleton heart, bidding 4♠ would be sane.

This is a rare situation where a bid does not show a good hand. East should realize from the auction that West is weak. Importantly, note that North-South may push on to 5♥, in which case you may set them a trick and that will be a super result.

East Deals + East-West Vulnerable

WEST	EAST
♠ J742	♠ Q93
♥ Q43	♥ AJ7
♦ K53	♦ AQJ
♣ Q75	♣ K962

WEST	NORTH	EAST	SOUTH
		1NT	Pass
?			

AFTER A FIFTEEN to seventeen point 1NT bid from East, West has to decide whether to bid or pass. What is your choice?

WEST	NORTH	EAST	SOUTH
		1NT	All pass

The key is the quality of the eight points West has. I have all too often held an opening 1NT hand and been raised to 2NT with something like the West hand. The compliment is appreciated but I would rather take seven tricks in a 1NT contract than in a 2NT or 3NT contract.

It is not that West has only eight points. It's that they are lousy points, with vile shape and no spot cards.

As the hands are, East has only six sure tricks. If East isn't lucky 1NT might go down, even though declarer has 25 points to work with.

Here are two layouts that take advantage of a little rearranging.

WEST	EAST
♠ J 7 4	♠ Q 9 3
♥ Q 4 3	♥ A J 7
♦ K 6 5 3 2	♦ A Q J
♣ Q 7	♣ K 9 6 2

In this layout, I gave West two more little diamonds. It is not farfetched that 3NT can be made now. It is still an uphill struggle but it can be done. Add to the equation that the opening lead might be helpful and 3NT becomes even better.

WEST	EAST
♠ J 10 4 2	♠ Q 9 3
♥ Q 10 3	♥ A J 7
♦ K 10 3	♦ A Q J
♣ Q 10 5	♣ K 9 6 2

In this layout, I gave West the same high cards and shape but added in the four ten-spots. These do wonders for the hand.

Without the ♠10, declarer might get one trick, and he could get two tricks but that would be very lucky.

With the ♠10, East can get two tricks for sure. Easy stuff.

Without the ♥10, East can get two easy heart tricks but seldom can he get three.

With the ♥10, East has only to take the heart finesse, which wins three heart tricks if North has the king.

The ♦10 does nothing for the hand because your side already has all the other high diamonds.

Without the ♣10, East can get one sure trick but a second trick will be elusive.

With the ♣10, two tricks are easy and a third is not that unlikely if East can guess which defender has the jack.

All in all, adding four tens to the West hand adds nearly three tricks to the combined hands.

RULE

Do not count points only. Count all the spot cards too and be sure to consider long suits. They can offer you extra tricks that balanced hands do not.

SPECIAL HINT

If you have eight points and a 4-3-3-3 hand, you may or may not choose to raise. Spot cards are important, as you saw from the previous discussion. Having a five-card suit is also a big addition to your values.

Did you know that a 4-4-3-2 hand is better than a 4-3-3-3 hand for play in notrump? If you have 4-3-3-3 shape, you have only one four-card suit to offer an additional trick. If you have 4-4-3-2 shape, you have two suits to offer as sources of extra tricks.

Don't go too far with this thought. If you have 4-4-4-1, having three suits to go after is nice but the singleton suggests that the opponents have a good suit to attack. It's a tradeoff.

WEST	EAST
♠ Q J 3	♠ K 9 8 2
♥ Q J 6 4 3	♥ A 2
♦ 9 7 6	♦ Q J 5
♣ 3 2	♣ K J 9 8

WEST	NORTH	EAST	SOUTH
		1♣	Pass
1♥	Pass	1♠	Pass
?			

THE BIDDING HAS gone in routine fashion with East opening 1♣, West responding 1♥, and East bidding 1♠.

How should West continue?

WEST	NORTH	EAST	SOUTH
		1♣	Pass
1♥	Pass	1♠	All pass

West's pass is best because 1♠ looks better than any other spot. 1NT has warts all over it. West has flimsy hearts, minimum points, and no supporting tens and nines.

1NT will be uphill all the way unless East has a perfect hand for it.

Rebidding hearts is too horrible to contemplate. East could have one heart and likely would pass 2♥. What is left is passing, and that's the winner. This is hardly a bad thing. East should be able to get a club ruff or two, and those are tricks that you can't get in any other contract.

A good rule of thumb is when you are minimum and the bidding isn't going anywhere good, get out of the auction as soon as you see a resting spot. 1♠ fits that description perfectly.

QUICKIE

♠ K Q 4   ♠ A 8 6 5 2

How often will you take five tricks at notrump with this suit?

The answer is that you need a 3-2 break, and that will happen 68% of the time. A useful percentage to know. Knowing this, how likely is it that South can make 6NT?

♠ A K
♥ 8 7 3
♦ A Q 7 6 4
♣ K 5 3

♠ Q 7
♥ K 9 4
♦ K 3 2
♣ A Q 7 6 2

This is not as good a slam as you might think. The point count is almost enough. But the ♠Q doesn't help. Even if you get a heart trick, you still need both minor suits to divide 3-2. The odds on that turn out to be 68% for the diamond break and 68% for the club break. Multiply these together and the chances for slam are around 46%.

West Deals   +   East-West Vulnerable

WEST	EAST
♠ 5	♠ 10 8 7 4 3
♥ K Q 9 7 6 3	♥ A 8
♦ K 3	♦ A Q 5 2
♣ K Q 8 3	♣ 10 2

WEST	NORTH	EAST	SOUTH
1♥	Pass	1♠	Pass
2♥	Pass	?	

THE AUCTION STARTS normally enough. West bids 1♥ and East correctly responds with 1♠. West rebids his six-card heart suit. What should East bid?

- East has a reasonable hand.
- East doesn't have enough to bid 2NT.
- East should not bid 2♠. That bid promises six cards.
- East might pass but he does have two aces, a potential ruffing value, and a potentially nice card in the ♦Q.

His correct bid is 'none of the above'. East knows that West has six hearts. If West has five hearts, there are other bids he can make. If West has a balanced hand, he can usually rebid 1NT. If West has four clubs or four diamonds, he can usually bid two of that minor. His rebidding 2♥ is a very strong statement that he has six of them. He might have seven.

East should raise to 3♥. Facing a six-card suit, two-card support is fine for a raise as long as you have the needed values. West, with 6-4 shape and generally good points, is happy to bid 4♥.

North Deals + North-South Vulnerable

	WEST	EAST	
♠	K Q 8	♠ 7 6 3	
♥	A J 10 8 6	♥ K Q 5	
♦	Q 8 3	♦ K 7 4 2	
♣	J 3	♣ K 9 4	

WEST	NORTH	EAST	SOUTH
	Pass	Pass	Pass
1♥	1♠	?	

WEST OPENS 1♥ in fourth seat. North, who passed originally, comes in with 1♠. How should East show his good heart support?

WEST	NORTH	EAST	SOUTH
	Pass	Pass	Pass
1♥	1♠	2♣	Pass
2♥	Pass	?	

One of my favorite conventions is the Drury convention. It allows you to show support for your partner's third- and fourth-seat opening bids without automatically pushing the bidding to the three level.

Not well-recognized as an advantage of Drury is that it also lets you bid games and slams more efficiently because opener gets information about partner's support at an economical level.

On this hand, East has a perfect Drury hand, which means his correct bid is 2♣, showing about ten points with heart support.

This support can be three or four cards, but never two. Bidding Drury with only two-card support will ruin all of the good things this convention can do for you.

Note that the auction here is competitive. North overcalled 1♠. I have East using the Drury convention. Actually, Drury is at its best in competition because it allows responder to show his hand. That allows opener to go to the three level or higher if he has a good hand, and it gives the partnership the option of not competing if opener has a sour hand.

Opener rebids 2♥. In this form of Drury (called Reverse Drury), a rebid of the major by opener says he has no interest in game. Still, the East hand is pretty good. Should East make just one more game try of some sort?

WEST	NORTH	EAST	SOUTH
	Pass	Pass	Pass
1♥	1♠	2♣	Pass
2♥	All pass		

East should pass. He has three good trumps, and he has two side kings as opposed to a hodge-podge of queens and jacks. All nice cards. But they are not enough. Even if East had four hearts, stopping in 2♥ would be correct.

Remember, East said he had in the range of a limit raise and opener said he had no interest.

Considering that West can open 1♥ with some nine- or ten-point hands in third seat, passing is the clear winner. If your partner is likely to open 1♥ with four cards, then passing 2♥ is all the better.

POSTMORTEM

Looking at the two hands, you can see that there are six potential losers. If South has the ♣A, 2♥ may go down. Yes, there are some elimination plays that might work, but going down in 2♥ is not impossible. If East had taken liberties and gone to 3♥, the result would very likely be a minus score. This is true even though West has a normal but minimum opening bid. He could have from one to four points less.

East Deals + North-South Vulnerable

	WEST		EAST
♠	A Q 9 2	♠	K J 8 4
♥	5 3	♥	A K 10 6
♦	9 8 7	♦	K J
♣	A J 9 6	♣	K Q 5

WEST	NORTH	EAST	SOUTH
		2NT	Pass
3♣	Pass	3♥	Pass
3NT	Pass	4♠	Pass
4NT	Pass	5♥	Pass
6♠	All pass		

THIS IS A test of your partnership understandings and of West's judgment. East opens 2NT, showing 20–21 points. West bids Stayman, looking for a major.

East bids 3♥, which is the normal thing to do when you have both majors. West has a pretty hand with no obvious bid. He knows the partnership has 32 points maximum and there is no known fit yet so he reasonably stops in 3NT.

East, having both majors and knowing that West wouldn't bid Stayman without a four-card major, bids 4♠.

West suddenly has a very good hand. He bids 4NT. This can only be keycard for spades. West would not use Stayman without a major so 4NT as a natural bid makes no sense. East obliges by showing two keycards without the ♠Q. West bids the slam. Once a fit is found, the partnership has a couple of additional distributional points available.

Now East has to make it.

East Deals + North-South Vulnerable

	WEST		EAST
♠	7 4	♠	A 8 6 2
♥	Q 8 7 3	♥	K 10 6
♦	Q 6	♦	K 8 7 2
♣	Q J 8 7 3	♣	K 6

WEST	NORTH	EAST	SOUTH
		1♦	Pass
1♥	1♠	Dbl	Pass
2♣	All pass		

THIS IS A discussion hand relating to support doubles. The auction starts normally with East bidding 1♦ and West 1♥. When North overcalls 1♠ East can, if he wants, raise hearts. He can do this in two ways.

1. Bid 2♥. If using support doubles, a raise to 2♥ shows four-card support. East can't do that if using this convention.
2. Double. If using support doubles, a double of an overcall which is lower than two of your trump suit shows exactly three-card support.

It's possible that opener will have a very good hand with three-card support. If so, he doubles to show the support and then makes further bids to show the extra values.

This hand is acceptable for a support double. It is in the minimum family so will not bid again unless West makes forcing bids.

This brings the bidding back to West. West has to bid again. He can't pass 1♠, doubled. West can do a couple of things.

He can bid 2♥, playing in a known four-three fit, which is not appealing with this poor a trump suit.

Or he can bid 2♣ in an effort to play in clubs.

For 2♣ to be a winning bid, it is necessary to define it properly. Experience has shown that playing this bid to show a weak hand with a good suit is best. It denies a five-card heart suit (the major your side is bidding) and it denies a good hand. 2♣ offers a place to play the contract. Opener may bid again but if he does, it will be with the awareness that responder has a hand like this one.

On this hand, East passes 2♣ and that becomes the contract. It turns out that there is no good contract because there is no eight-card fit, but 2♣ is better than 1NT and probably better than 2♥.

POSTMORTEM

There are other bids West can make after East's support double. Here is a brief discussion of them.

WEST	NORTH	EAST	SOUTH
		1♦	Pass
1♥	1♠	Dbl	Pass
?			

1NT A minimum hand (6–10) with nothing more appealing. It promises (more or less) a spade stopper. 1NT is not forcing.

2♦ Going back to opener's suit is natural and not forcing.

2♠ This is a game-forcing cuebid. Responder can have lots of hands, including five hearts.

2NT Invitational. 11–12 balanced points.

3♣	A jump to 3♣ is also invitational. A useful treatment.
3♦	A normal limit raise.
3♥	Invitational with five hearts.

These bids give responder many options. Most of them are natural.

South Deals + No One Vulnerable

WEST	EAST
♠ A Q 10 7 5	♠ 8 2
♥ K Q J 8	♥ A 9 5
♦ 3 2	♦ 9 5 4
♣ 7 3	♣ A 9 8 4 2

WEST	NORTH	EAST	SOUTH
			1♦
1♠	2♦	Pass	Pass
2♥	All pass		

SOUTH BIDS 1♦ and West overcalls 1♠. Doubling with this hand is a bad idea. East may bid clubs. He may bid notrump. And in either case, West won't be able to bid spades to show five since doubling and bidding a suit shows a bigger hand.

So West bids 1♠, correctly. East has modest values but he has no safe bid. He passes, as he should.

When it gets back to West, he considers that the opponents have not shown great values so he bids 2♥. This is not an over-bid at all. East could have four hearts, and East-West making a partscore is very possible.

Here is a question for East. It is a very important question.

What is West's distribution?

If you are not sure, here is a backup question.

Can West have five spades and five hearts?

Whatever your answer is, prove it.

The answer is that West does not have 5-5 shape. If he had 5-5 shape he would have used the Michaels cuebid (assuming you use Michaels). He would have bid 2♦ over 1♦ to show a 5-5 hand.

North Deals + North-South Vulnerable

WEST	EAST
♠ A Q 7 4	♠ K J 9
♥ 8 4 3	♥ A K 10 9
♦ J 10 8	♦ K 7 6 3
♣ 10 8 3	♣ 9 4

WEST	NORTH	EAST	SOUTH
	1♣	Dbl	Pass
1♠	2♣	Pass	Pass
?			

EAST DOUBLES 1♣ and West responds 1♠. West should be fairly happy with his hand since he might have had a much weaker hand. It's always nice to have a good four-card suit to bid when partner makes a takeout double.

When North rebids 2♣, East passes, and West is up again. Do you think the West hand is worth another bid? If so, which bid is correct?

WEST	NORTH	EAST	SOUTH
	1♣	Dbl	Pass
1♠	2♣	Pass	Pass
2♠	3♣	All pass	

West does something odd. He rebids his four-card spade suit. This is not a classic case of rebidding a suit. What West is doing is not showing extra length, but extra points. His 1♠ bid promised zero to eight points. West has seven. He has a maximum for his call.

Look at it this way. Say South had raised to 2♣. West would (should) have bid 2♠ to say he had four spades and about seven points.

Since West's first bid didn't show any values, he had lots in reserve to bid a second time.

When North bid 3♣, West was comfortable in passing since he had shown his hand with his earlier bids. This was a very good performance by West.

POSTMORTEM

Note the East hand. He made a takeout double. West bid 1♠ and East correctly passed North's 2♣ bid. East has a nice minimum and most important of all, has only three spades.

VERY IMPORTANT

When West bid 2♠ and North continued to 3♣, East did a good thing. He passed. Yes, East has a smidgen more than a minimum, but that is not sufficient to bid.

The key to East's silence is this. West could have bid 2♠ on the first round. He did not. West's hand has a maximum of about seven or eight points if he has four spades, and a maximum of six or seven points if he has five spades.

This doesn't add up to East-West making 3♠. East did well to pass and not hang West for doing a good thing.

As you can see, East-West have chances to defeat 3♣ and they have little chance of making 3♠.

As the cards lie, West can't make 3♠ and might go down in two. 3♣ is down one.

HAND
83

	WEST	EAST
♠	A J 10 6 3	♠ 9 7
♥	3	♥ A K J 7 4
♦	A J 4	♦ 7 6 3
♣	Q 8 7 6	♣ A J 9

WEST	NORTH	EAST	SOUTH
1♠	Pass	2♥	Pass
2♠	Pass	3♣	Pass
4♣	Pass	4♠	All pass

THIS IS AN example of a bidding trick that went awry. It happens. I imagine you have seen this one before and did not enjoy it very much.

West starts with 1♠ and East bids 2♥.

West rebids 2♠. Do you agree with 2♠?

The reason for bidding 2♠ instead of 3♣ is that going to the three level promises a better hand. A lot of players 'know' this but they do not honor it at the table. They bid 3♣ and wonder why the auction went sour. Another possible bid by West is 2NT. Personally, I won't do this with a singleton in partner's suit. He will expect me to have two and will bid with that in mind.

East now bids 3♣. Do you agree?

This is a good bid. East can't bid notrump and rebidding hearts promises six. Also, since a 2♠ rebid promises only five spades, East can't raise them just yet. 3♣ is a fourth suit kind of bid, one you have to make up when other bids don't make sense.

West bids 4♣. It is kind of hard to disagree with this bid. Four-card support is too much to ignore. I suppose that West could bid 3NT now but let's face it. No bid feels 'right' here. After all, East might actually have real clubs.

East bids 4♠. Do you agree?

This is as good a bid as East has. Here are his choices:

1. Pass. Hardly logical. This would be a strange action. Since there is one sensible bid available, it is not as if East has nothing to do.
2. 4♥. Silly. West denied three hearts so the best East can hope for is to find West with two of them. He might have one. If East bids 4♥ he risks playing it there, a likely possibility.
3. 5♣. A wild shot. Could work, however. I won't disown this bid entirely.
4. 4♠. This is your most likely game. It may not make but it will have some chances. One nice quality of this bid is that it shows two spades. East would have raised 2♠ to 3♠ earlier with three.

POSTMORTEM

This kind of auction happens in Standard bidding and in Two Over One bidding too. When responder goes to the two level and on the next round is not sure what to do, he often bids a three-card suit as a waiting bid. Once in awhile, the events of this hand occur and it is touch and go if you will survive.

West Deals   +   East-West Vulnerable

	WEST	EAST	
	♠ K 7 4	♠ 6 5 3	
	♥ A Q 7 4 3 2	♥ —	
	♦ 5	♦ Q J 9 7 6	
	♣ K 10 6	♣ A Q J 8 5	

WEST	NORTH	EAST	SOUTH
1♥	Pass	1NT	Pass
2♥	Pass	?	

WHAT SHOULD EAST do?

In hand 70, I discussed a bid known as 'the impossible 2♠ bid'. This hand shows an interesting variation.

When West opens 1♥ and rebids 2♥, showing six or more cards, East has an unpleasant choice. He can pass but he should fear that there is a better contract. A 2♠ bid here says that he has nine or more points* and at least 5-5 in the minors. West is asked to choose a minor.

Here, West prefers clubs so he bids 3♣.

Without this convention, East would not be able to show both minors. Most likely, East would pass and hope for the best.

Reminder. If East has a lousy hand, it is best to pass 2♥.

*Something important. East didn't make a two-over-one response so he is marked with less than an opening bid.

WEST	NORTH	EAST	SOUTH
1♥	Pass	1NT	Pass
2♥	Pass	2♠	Pass
3♣	All pass		

West Deals + No One Vulnerable

WEST	EAST
♠ K Q 2	♠ 8 5
♥ A K J 10 5	♥ Q 8 7 4
♦ A Q 2	♦ K J 4
♣ A K	♣ J 8 6 2

WEST	NORTH	EAST	SOUTH
2♣	Pass	2♦*	Pass
2♥	Pass	3♥	Pass
4NT	Pass	5♣	Pass
5♦	Pass	6♦	Pass
6♥	All pass		

*WAITING

WEST STARTS WITH the big one, 2♣, and gets the expected 2♦ response. West can choose from bidding some number of notrump and bidding hearts. If West rebids 3NT, showing points, East will have no idea how to continue no matter what his hand.

2♥ is a better choice because it keeps all suits open. East may have something he can bid. If he has nothing, he can bid 3♣, the second negative showing a terrible hand.

East raises to 3♥. He does not raise to 4♥. A raise to 3♥ promises something. A raise to 4♥ shows a very weak hand with no ace, no king, and no shape. If East raises to 4♥, West should pass since he knows he is missing an ace and the ♦K as well, in addition to the possibility that there is a trump loser.

When East bids 3♥, West can count on some values and he bids 4NT. East shows no keycards. West might risk 6♥ anyway but he can bid 5♦, asking about the ♥Q. East's 6♦ bid shows the ♥Q and the ♦K.

West chooses to play in 6♥. Note that West does not bid 6NT. 6♥ is the better contract since West can ruff a spade in dummy should that be necessary.

HAND 86

	WEST		EAST
♠	A Q J 8 6	♠	K 9 5 4 3
♥	8 6 5 3	♥	9
♦	4 3	♦	Q 9 8 7 5
♣	10 8	♣	J 7

WEST	NORTH	EAST	SOUTH
			2♣
2♠	3♦	?	

EAST HOLDS A lousy hand and is not too happy to hear South open 2♣. But things get brighter in a hurry. West overcalls 2♠ and North bids 3♦.

How should East bid here?

East should realize that North-South must have something good in one of the unbid suits, if not notrump. He could bid 4♠ but that leaves South room to bid a suit at the five level or even to bid 4NT, asking for aces.

The key is that East must find the right bid. Any overcall by West was likely to upset their delicate auction. The 2♠ bid has already cost North-South some bidding room. If East bids 4♠ or 5♠, North-South will lose a lot more room. I like 5♠ for the reasons mentioned above.

Looking at the East hand, you can imagine that West might make 2♠, which means that even if North-South only have a game, the cost of bidding 5♠ will be 500. This is a good result since they are vulnerable.

Here's the auction that North-South have to contend with:

WEST	NORTH	EAST	SOUTH
			2♣
2♠	3♦	5♠	Dbl
Pass	?		

Here is the complete hand:

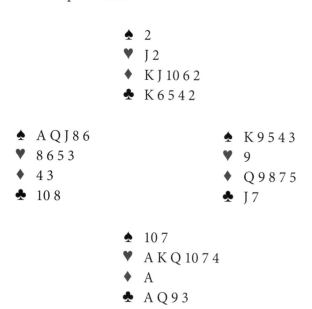

```
                      ♠ 2
                      ♥ J 2
                      ♦ K J 10 6 2
                      ♣ K 6 5 4 2

      ♠ A Q J 8 6                      ♠ K 9 5 4 3
      ♥ 8 6 5 3                        ♥ 9
      ♦ 4 3                            ♦ Q 9 8 7 5
      ♣ 10 8                           ♣ J 7

                      ♠ 10 7
                      ♥ A K Q 10 7 4
                      ♦ A
                      ♣ A Q 9 3
```

POSTMORTEM

Poor South never got to bid his hearts. For obvious reasons,
South hated to bid a slam and North was not happy removing the
double without a known fit. If West doesn't bid, South will show
his suits and North will bid a slam somewhere along the line.

Note that the bidding is not necessarily over. If North-South
bid a slam, East may choose to bid 6♠.

East Deals + North-South Vulnerable

EAST

♠ 6 4
♥ 10 9 8 7 5 3
♦ K 8 3
♣ 9 4

WEST	NORTH	EAST	SOUTH
1♣	1♦	?	

IN HAND 73, I introduced weak jump shifts. In that discussion, I showed hands where opener bid one of a suit, the next player passed, and responder made a weak jump shift to two of a new suit, showing a weak hand with a six-card suit.

You can use these bids after an overcall and after a takeout double. As long as you can jump to the two level in a new suit, it remains a weak bid with similar values as before. The point of this article is to show the weak jump shift in competition.

Be aware that making a weak jump shift when the opponents have entered the bidding is not as safe as when they haven't bid. However, it is still important for you to bid because this is your only chance to contribute to the auction. Be brave and bid if you have a glimmer of a reason. You will get some horrible results. You will get some good results. If you don't abuse the standards needed for a preemptive jump shift, you'll come out ahead.

When your RHO overcalls:

On the hand above, I suggest East bid 2♥. The suit is weak but the solid sequence is a gentle plus. You have the ♦K behind the bidder, so it's a winner. Your bid is a small annoyance to South. He can't bid 1♠ and he can't bid 1NT and he can't raise to 2♦. For you to get a very bad result, the opponents will have to double you and then set you two tricks. In the meantime, you will earn a number of small triumphs that will add up. On rare hands you might reach a making game.

The point of this discussion is that if your RHO comes in at the one level and you have bidding room to make a jump shift to the two level, you should consider it. That overcall isn't a big threat. If you would have made a weak jump shift after a pass by RHO, you should make the same bid (room permitting) after an overcall by RHO.

Here is a repeat of the methods I recommended in an earlier hand. Consider this a refresher on these methods. Go back to hand 73 for more details.

WEST	NORTH	EAST	SOUTH
1♣	1♦	2♥	Pass
2NT	Pass	?	

If opener has a good hand with a fit and wants to know how good responder's hand is, he can bid 2NT to ask for information. 2NT is forcing. Responder answers via four artificial steps.

3♣   I have a minimum hand and a bad suit.
3♦   I have a minimum hand and a decent suit.
3♥   I have a good hand but my suit is bad.
3♠   I have a good hand and I have a good suit.

♠   7 3
♥   10 9 8 7 5 3
♦   K 8 3
♣   9 4

Bid 3♣. Minimum hand with a weak suit.

♠ 7 3
♥ K 10 8 7 6 3
♦ 8 3
♣ 7 6 4

Bid 3♦. This shows a minimum hand with a decent suit.

♠ 7 6 3
♥ J 10 8 7 5 3
♦ A 3
♣ 10 8

Bid 3♥. This shows a good hand and a poor suit.

♠ 8 3
♥ K 10 8 7 6 4
♦ 9 6 5
♣ Q 5

Bid 3♠. Your suit is good and your hand is also maximum. In the context used here where you have already claimed a weak hand, this one is good.

When your RHO makes a takeout double:

WEST	NORTH	EAST	SOUTH
1♣	Dbl	?	

If your RHO makes a takeout double, a jump by you to the two level shows a poor hand but not a lousy hand. You should have a decent suit such as QJ9864. The doubler has promised he has three or four cards in this suit. In comparison, if your RHO overcalled 1♦ you can jump in a weaker suit since you don't have to worry as much about a bad break. Very important: If you are vulnerable, be even more careful about your preemptive jump shifts. Being vulnerable, down two undoubled can be a miserable result.

If you are not vulnerable and RHO doubles:

♠ Q 9 8 6 5 3
♥ 4 3
♦ 5 4 3
♣ J 10

Pass. You might have bid 2♠ if RHO had passed. His double is a warning. Don't bid 2♠ here. You have a wretched suit which is a warning on auctions where RHO made a takeout double. Hands which might have been worth a bid when RHO passed or overcalled do not always qualify for a bid after a takeout double.

♠ K J 10 9 8 5
♥ 5 4 3
♦ 4 3
♣ 6 5

Bid 2♠. This is an excellent suit, which is a big requirement when bidding after a takeout double. Considering that RHO made a takeout double, this is a solid minimum hand.

If you are vulnerable and RHO doubles:

♠ K Q 10 9 8 2
♥ J 3
♦ 5 2
♣ 8 6 4

2♠ is sane here given the combination of being vulnerable and faced with a takeout double.

There's no need to overdo these bids. You want to follow agreed standards so that your partner will know what to expect. You will see players making weak jump shifts with truly bad hands and sometimes with only a five-card suit. Don't do these things. When you set one of these players 800 you will see why.

North Deals   +   East-West Vulnerable

WEST	EAST
♠ 8	♠ Q J 6
♥ 10 4 2	♥ K Q 5
♦ 10 7	♦ A Q 3 2
♣ A K 10 7 6 5 3	♣ Q J 4

WEST	NORTH	EAST	SOUTH
	1♣	1NT	3♠
?			

WEST HAS A decision to make after South's 3♠ bid. No one asked what it meant but I can tell you that it was a weak bid. If South had a good hand, he would have doubled 1NT. What should West bid now?

WEST	NORTH	EAST	SOUTH
	1♣	1NT	3♠
3NT	All pass		

This is the practical solution. West has too many losers to risk 5♣ but he has enough tricks that 3NT could be easy. As it is, 3NT is cold.

POSTMORTEM

Say South had bid 4♠ instead of 3♠. What should West bid now?

The answer is that West should bid 4NT. This is a natural bid. It does not ask for aces. Given your partner has a strong notrump hand, 4NT will usually be your best spot. It turns out that you will probably make 5♣ but 4NT is also likely.

	WEST	EAST
♠	A Q 7	♠ 8 6 5 2
♥	K 7 6 3	♥ Q J 4
♦	7 3	♦ Q J 4
♣	K J 10 4	♣ A 8 7

WEST	NORTH	EAST	SOUTH
1♣	1♠	?	

NOW AND THEN, you get a hand like the one East has. East has a decent ten-count which means it rates to be worth a bid, but it does not offer a sensible bid. Do you have a thought on this?

My thoughts are that this is an ugly situation. Here are your choices.

1. 1NT. Obviously flawed. You don't have a stopper. Worse, you might be able to make some number of notrump from partner's side of the table.

2. Double. A negative double makes some sense because you have enough extra values, but it too is missing a critical element, the fourth heart. While this bid might survive, you will put worries in the back of your partner's mind. He may be afraid to compete after one of your negative doubles for fear that you don't have the promised length in one of the majors.

3. 2♣. This bid is flawed because you don't have four cards in clubs. I actually like it, though, relative to the other choices, because it keeps the bidding low. If you get higher, it is because your partner chose to go higher and

it will probably be all right. Of the four bids mentioned on this list, I view this one as the least flawed.

4. Pass. This could work, too. However, a big problem comes up if your partner reopens with a double. Whatever you bid, your partner won't play you for ten points.

I present this hand without really giving you a solution. Perhaps that is because there is no solution.

As noted, I would be only mildly unhappy with a raise to 2♣. If my partner has only three of them, then I look silly, but I am prepared to apologize.

WEST		EAST	
♠ A J 3 2		♠ 9 5	
♥ 6 4 3		♥ K Q 10 8	
♦ K Q 8 7		♦ A 10 6 5 2	
♣ A 10		♣ 8 3	

WEST	NORTH	EAST	SOUTH
1♦	2♣	Dbl	3♣
?			

WEST STARTS WITH 1♦ and has to decide whether his hand is worth bidding 3♠ when the auction becomes competitive.

How do you feel about it? Should West bid or pass here?

WEST	NORTH	EAST	SOUTH
1♦	2♣	Dbl	3♣
3♠	Pass	4♦	Pass
?			

You have to be very aggressive in these bidding situations. When you have a fit, you either show it or you lose it. If West had a minimum hand, passing would be OK because if East had enough to make 3♣ he would probably bid again. Here, West has good cards and perhaps a queen more than a minimum so bidding 3♠ is OK.

What do you think East is doing? Should West pass 4♦ or is there a bid worth making?

East must have hearts but not spades. And he must have more than a minimum negative double because he was prepared to go back to diamonds at a higher level when West bid spades.

His hand rates to look like a limit raise but with four hearts too. The West hand is not quite good enough to bid 5♦.

POSTMORTEM

I mentioned in the discussion that if opener had a minimum hand he should strive to show a major. This is especially true at the two level.

WEST	NORTH	EAST	SOUTH
1♣	1♥	Dbl	2♥
?			

It is hard to imagine a hand with four spades that would not bid 2♠ at this point.

♠ Q 8 7 3
♥ K J 2
♦ Q J 4
♣ K J 7

This hand is bad enough to pass. But it is tempting to bid.

♠ Q J 8 2
♥ A 4 3
♦ K 3
♣ Q 10 9 4

This hand has only twelve points but I would suggest bidding 2♠ with it. This hand has better spades, better shape, and overall, is a better hand than the previous one.

Going back to the original discussion:

WEST	NORTH	EAST	SOUTH
1♦	2♣	Dbl	3♣
3♠	Pass	4♦	All pass

If East happens to have enough to bid game, he has to bid the full value of his hand.

♠ K 5
♥ K Q 10 8
♦ A 10 6 5 2
♣ 8 3

East correctly started with a negative double, looking for a heart contract. When West bid 3♠, East should bid 5♦, not 4♦. My usual observation here is that if North hadn't bid 2♣, this hand would have been much easier to bid.

	EAST	
	♠ 9 8 3 2	
	♥ J 6 3 2	
	♦ J 10 8 3	
	♣ 6	

WEST	NORTH	EAST	SOUTH
1NT	Pass	?	

EAST HAS A terrible hand facing a strong 1NT opening bid. Should he pass 1NT?

There is a version of Stayman that makes excellent sense. It is called Drop Dead Stayman (among other names). East can bid Stayman without promising any values. His intent is to show a weak hand by passing on his next turn, or perhaps making a second bid that is defined as a weak bid.

On this hand West bids 2♦. Since West doesn't have a major, it is likely that West has diamonds. He may have four of them, he could have five of them. In any event East passes 2♦, which rates to be better than 1NT.

Using this version of Stayman means you never, ever have to pass partner's 1NT bid with a singleton club. You always have a way to escape. Here's the layout:

WEST	EAST
♠ A 7	♠ 9 8 3 2
♥ K Q 10	♥ J 6 3 2
♦ A K 4	♦ J 10 8 3
♣ 10 5 4 3 2	♣ 6

Useful thought: If your opponents use Drop Dead Stayman and end in 2♦, consider leading a trump.

HAND	East Deals + East-West Vulnerable
92	

	WEST	EAST
♠	A 7 5 3	♠ K Q 4
♥	J 9 8 2	♥ K Q 5 3
♦	10 8	♦ J 7
♣	A J 4	♣ Q 9 8 3

WEST	NORTH	EAST	SOUTH
		1♣	1♦
?			

WEST HAS AN easy bid after South's 1♦ overcall. Do you agree?

WEST	NORTH	EAST	SOUTH
		1♣	1♦
Dbl	3♦	Pass	Pass
?			

West's negative double promises both majors. Usually you have four-four although with some minimum hands, you might have five-four shape. You might judge it important to show both majors while you can.

When North makes his preemptive 3♦ bid the bidding comes back to you.

Is your hand good enough for another bid? If you decide it is, what would that bid be?

WEST	NORTH	EAST	SOUTH
		1♣	1♦
Dbl	3♦	Pass	Pass
Dbl	Pass	3♥	Pass
?			

East seems to be on the same wavelength. If he thought your double was for penalty, there could be a disaster. Note that East did not bid 3♥ on the previous round. East needs a fair hand to bid 3♥. This hand is worth an opening bid but it is hardly worth a bid at the three level.

Should West go on or should he let East play in 3♥?

WEST	NORTH	EAST	SOUTH
		1♣	1♦
Dbl	3♦	Pass	Pass
Dbl	Pass	3♥	All pass

West passes and says a little prayer that 3♥ is not too high. East did pass over 3♦ so he is marked with a minimum-range hand. Bidding 4♥ indicates that West has a short memory.

POSTMORTEM

3♥ is a good spot. Not perfect, but good.

I noted in the discussion that it is important for your partnership to know what this double means. I also noted that if East passed the double, there could be trouble.

This isn't entirely true. East, assuming he knows what the double means, is entitled to pass if he thinks 3♦ will go down. He knows that West has ten or more points and he knows that West has four-four in the majors. If the East hand doesn't have a major suit, he may elect to defend.

WEST	EAST
♠ A 7 5 3	♠ K Q 4
♥ J 9 8 2	♥ K Q 5
♦ 10 8	♦ J 7 3
♣ A J 4	♣ Q 9 8 3

If East had this hand, he might reasonably decide to pass 3♦, doubled. The idea is that with no fit, it might be hard to impossible to make anything. This is kind of true here. There is no good contract for East-West.

On defense, there is the potential for three spade tricks, two heart tricks, and two club tricks. If the defense can get five of these tricks, they will get a plus score.

Personally, I would be content to pass with the East hand at matchpoints but would hate the hand if I was playing IMPs.

Perhaps this particular East hand isn't worth an opening bid. This is a quizzical note, not a definitive statement.

ONE LAST COMMENT

Players today are much more active in the bidding than they were twenty years ago. They have more tools to use and they do love to use them. The weak jump raise in competition is one of them. North's jump to 3♦ was a preemptive bid promising four trumps and a little shape. Five or six points is normal.

I have seen some pretty pushy preemptive raises lately. You have to judge your opponents but if you believe one of them to be a wild sort, the chances of your setting 3♦, doubled, will be better than against a solid citizen, of whom there are fewer today than yesterday.

West Deals ✛ North-South Vulnerable

	WEST		EAST
♠	K J	♠	Q 10 8 6 5 2
♥	A Q 7 3	♥	5
♦	K Q 6	♦	10 5
♣	J 9 7 3	♣	A Q 8 6

WEST	NORTH	EAST	SOUTH
1NT	2♥	4♥	Pass
4♠	All pass		

THIS IS JUST a system thought. West opens a normal 1NT and North bids 2♥. What should East bid?

First, East has to decide what his hand is worth. Is it worth bidding game? I would guess yes.

If so, you need to choose a bid.

The one shown above is Texas. East's 4♥ bid asks West to bid 4♠.

POSTMORTEM

Some bidding moments are not obvious. If you held the East hand would you currently know that 4♥ was a Texas bid? This is a good thing to discuss with your partner.

There is a quirk that you must address. Some players play that these transfer bids apply only if the opponent bid 3♣ or lower. Some play these transfer bids no matter what RHO bids. For instance, if RHO bids 3♦, they may wish to play that 4♦ is a transfer to hearts and 4♥ is a transfer to spades.

Be very sure you agree on which variation you use.

West Deals   +   No One Vulnerable

WEST	EAST
♠ A K 10 6	♠ Q J 7
♥ 2	♥ 8 7
♦ 7 6 2	♦ A K 9 8 3
♣ A K 10 5 2	♣ 9 4 3

WEST	NORTH	EAST	SOUTH
1♣	2♥	?	

THIS AUCTION IS difficult from both sides of the table. West opens 1♣ and North makes a weak jump overcall of 2♥.

What in the world should East bid? Awkward. Here are East's choices.

1. Pass. Looking at this hand, you know it should bid something. What that something is remains to be determined.

2 3♣. Sometimes, raising your partner's minor suit, even with only three cards, is the best way to go. Three small is not my idea of good support so while I am willing to consider this bid, I am not making it until I am convinced it is best.

3 3♦. This just can't be right. Effectively, you are making a game-forcing bid. At best, you might get your partner to bid 3NT, but if he can't, his bid is likely to get you to the four level or higher. Even if he bids 3NT, there's no certainty he will make it.

4. Double. A negative double has to be on the list of choices. The hand has the obvious flaw of having only three spades. It does, however, have extra values. You could double with a couple of points less.

My choice is to double. You have extra values and the three spades you have are good ones. I would not make this bid with fewer points or worse spades.

♠ J 8 3
♥ 7 4
♦ A K 9 8 3
♣ Q 9 4

With this ten-point hand, I would lean towards raising clubs.

It is all very delicate. Feel free to get other opinions on this hand if you are not happy with mine. I'm prepared to agree with anything (almost anything) you say.

The auction continues:

WEST	NORTH	EAST	SOUTH
1♣	2♥	Dbl	3♥
?			

What should West bid?

West has an easier bid than East did. West just has to decide whether to bid 3♠ or 4♠. I vote for 4♠ for an important reason.

If you have followed the other hands in this book, you will recall that I said you should bid a major aggressively when partner makes a negative double. I would bid 3♠ with something less than this hand. Because of this, when you are close to bidding game, you should go ahead and do it. You will find some good news and some bad news.

The bad news is that there may be some bad distribution.

The good news is that you will know where the high cards are and should be able to play the hand as well as possible.

In 4♠, North leads the two top hearts. How should West play?

Discard a diamond on the second heart. You are not cold for 4♠ but this play allows you to keep trumps under control. The defenders can't shorten your trumps just yet.

The play can take many variations from here. Say they switch to diamonds. One possible line is to win it and play the top spades from dummy. Then duck a club, letting them have this trick. You hope you can get in and draw trump, and that the clubs will divide three-two.

You might like to consider how the play would go according to other defensive lines.

This is, after all, a discussion on bidding.

South Deals   +   No One Vulnerable

WEST	EAST
♠ A K 7 2	♠ 10 9 5 3
♥ Q J 8 2	♥ A 9 7 5
♦ J 3	♦ A 8 4
♣ Q 10 5	♣ K 3

WEST	NORTH	EAST	SOUTH
			1♦
Dbl	Pass	2♦	Pass
2♥	Pass	3♥	All pass

WHEN YOU MAKE a takeout double and your partner answers with a cuebid, is it forcing to game or can you stop in a partscore? This is just one more in the never-ending train of questions you have to face sooner or later.

It used to be that a cuebid was game forcing. Hands like this one finally changed the minds of most players. Look what happens when West doubles 1♦. East has a good hand that wants to ensure finding the best fit, but it's not good enough to force to game. East starts with a cuebid of 2♦. West bids hearts and East, now knowing that a 4-4 fit exists, raises to 3♥.

Now that a fit has been found, the cuebid loses its forcing nature. West can pass 3♥ and does so. If the bidding isn't able to find a 4-4 major suit fit, the partnership can also stay short of game. Using the cuebid this way assures you get to the best suit. Note that if you used 2♦ as game forcing, East wouldn't have a good bid. 2♦ would get you too high and if East jumped to 2♥ or 2♠, it might lead to playing in the wrong major suit.

East Deals   +   No One Vulnerable

WEST

♠ K 9 3
♥ A 9 7 6 3
♦ J 8 2
♣ 8 3

WEST	NORTH	EAST	SOUTH
		1♦	Pass
1♥	2♣	Dbl	3♣
?			

WEST RESPONDS 1♥ to East's 1♦ and the auction gets busy. North comes in with 2♣ and East doubles. This shows three-card support (support double) and says nothing about how strong his opening bid is.

South battles on to 3♣.

Should West bid 3♥ or pass?

WEST	NORTH	EAST	SOUTH
		1♦	Pass
1♥	2♣	Dbl	3♣
All pass			

It is probably right to pass. West has a balanced hand and he doesn't have that much to talk about. He does have five hearts, however.

The bigger reason for not bidding is that East has only three trumps. Eight-card fits are not nearly as useful as nine-card fits in the play, and they are much better for defense than hands with nine-card fits.

Followers of the law of total tricks (the Law) will appreciate this is true, but it's not necessary to follow the Law to come up with correct opinions. In this case, you are aware that your partner has three trumps.

If East had bid 2♥, not using support doubles, you would wonder if East had three trumps or four, and your decision-making would not be as accurate.

POSTMORTEM

WEST	EAST
♠ K 9 3	♠ J 8 5 2
♥ A 9 7 6 3	♥ K Q 5
♦ J 8 2	♦ A Q 5 4
♣ 8 3	♣ 10 6

In this layout, you have good chances to set 3♣ and you have marginal chances of making 3♥.

WEST	EAST
♠ K 9 3	♠ J 8 5
♥ A 9 7 6 3	♥ K Q 5 2
♦ J 8 2	♦ A Q 5 4
♣ 8 3	♣ 10 6

In this layout, I gave East one less spade and one more heart. Now your defensive chances are diminished a lot and your offense is improved by a similar amount.

I have no intention of reviewing the numbers used by Law users, but everyone knows the value of a ninth trump as compared with eight.

Note that if East had extras, he could bid again when 3♣ got back to him. East might have had one of these hands:

♠ A 8
♥ K Q 2
♦ A K Q 9 7
♣ 10 6 4

East can double 3♣ to show extra values.

♠ 8
♥ K J 4
♦ A K 10 9 6 3
♣ K J 7

East can bid 3♦ to show he has a good hand with a good suit. This is not forcing. Note how well this has worked out for East. He gets to show his strong hand and also that he has three-card support and good diamonds. What would you bid with this hand over 2♣ if you didn't use support doubles?

On a different auction, like this one, East can sometimes show a notrump hand.

WEST	NORTH	EAST	SOUTH
		1♦	Pass
1♥	2♣	Dbl	Pass
2♥	Pass	2NT	

♠ K 3
♥ Q 9 8
♦ A K J 10 7
♣ K Q 6

This sequence shows a hand that wanted to make a jump rebid of 2NT. East first showed heart support and then showed the rest of his values.

West Deals + No One Vulnerable

	WEST		EAST
♠	A J 7 6 3	♠	2
♥	Q 10 9	♥	K 8 6 3
♦	K J 3	♦	Q 7 6 4
♣	Q 8	♣	A 9 5 3

WEST	NORTH	EAST	SOUTH
1♠	Pass	1NT	Dbl
Pass	2♣	Dbl	All pass

THIS HAND IS for Two Over One bidders. West opened 1♠ and East made a forcing 1NT bid.

West has to rebid according to certain principles. Usually he rebids a six-card major or a lower-ranking four-card suit. Some of the time, as on this hand, he has to rebid a three-card minor.

However on this hand, there is a new variable. South just made a takeout double. In this circumstance, West no longer has to rebid. He can bid, but if he has an ordinary balanced hand, he is allowed to pass.

When North bid 2♣, East got to double it.

This would not have happened if West had blindly followed the system and bid 2♦ on his three-card suit. Because he did not rebid, North was forced to bid something and East got his hands on it.

POSTMORTEM

If West has shape, he will make his normal rebid. When he passes, the implication is that he has a balanced hand, and that made East's double even more worthwhile.

Yum.

West Deals   +   No One Vulnerable

	WEST		EAST
	♠ A K 8 3		♠ Q J 10 4
	♥ A Q J		♥ 9 8
	♦ A Q 10 2		♦ J 9 7
	♣ J 2		♣ A K 5 3

WEST	NORTH	EAST	SOUTH
2NT	Pass	3♣	Pass
3♠	Pass	4♥	Pass
?			

WEST OPENS 2NT, 20–21, and shows his spades in response to Stayman.

East's next bid is 4♥. Do you have any idea what that means? I will give you a hint since you may not have heard of this convention. Robert Goldman invented this bidding used after a 2NT opener. Today, almost everyone plays this convention.

Before I tell you what it is, give some thought to what it might be.

Here's the entire auction with explanations.

WEST	NORTH	EAST	SOUTH
2NT	Pass	3♣	Pass
3♠	Pass	4♥	Pass
4NT	Pass	5♦	Pass
5♥	Pass	6♣	Pass
6♠	All pass		

East was using the Goldman Slam Try. The 4♥ bid was an artificial bid saying that he liked spades and was interested in slam. West had a maximum with pretty good controls. He made a practical decision to use Blackwood.

He asked for aces and then asked for the queen of trumps with 5♥. East showed he had the queen of trumps and also the ♣K. West settled in 6♠, a very reasonable contract.

POSTMORTEM

If, on another layout, West had bid 3♥ in response to Stayman, East would bid 3♠ to show slam interest in hearts. The rule is that when opener shows a major suit, a bid in the other major shows a slam try in opener's major.

This convention has a hidden bonus. When responder bids the other major, he sets the trump suit. This allows him to bid 4NT next (if there is room) and opener will unconditionally know that it is keycard for the major.

WEST	NORTH	EAST	SOUTH
2NT	Pass	3♣	Pass
3♠	Pass	4♥	Pass
4♠	Pass	4NT	

If the bidding goes like this, East has a way to set spades as trump and then bid keycard if opener signs off. If you don't have this agreement, what is East to do? 4♣ is generally considered as natural, and even if you use it as Gerber, West doesn't know if there is a trump suit.

The Goldman Slam Try is such a good convention that almost all experienced players use it. This one has been passed the test of time.

HAND 99

	WEST	EAST
♠	K Q 7	10 8 2
♥	Q J 8 7 5	A K 6
♦	A 10 7 4	8 2
♣	7	K 10 9 6 4

WEST	NORTH	EAST	SOUTH
1♥	Pass	?	

HERE ARE TWO simple questions. Your partner opens 1♥.

1. What is your bid if playing Standard bidding?
2. What is your bid if playing Two Over One bidding?

1. *If using Standard bidding*
   What is your response?

   In Standard bidding, you have to bid a new suit at the two level and then return to hearts. Your bid here is 2♣. If partner bids 2♦, you bid 2♥. If he bids 2♥, you bid 3♥.

2. *If using Two Over One bidding*
   What is your response?

   In Two Over One bidding you don't have enough to bid 2♣ so you start with a forcing 1NT bid. Your intent is to bid 3♥ next on most auctions. This will tell your partner that you have a limit raise with three trumps.

The importance of this discussion is that no matter which method you play, you can not make a limit raise to 3♥. Jump raises promise four-card support. This is true in almost every bidding system I know. A 3♥ bid is lazy bridge. Your partner will bid as if you have four trumps. Having three trumps instead of four can be costly.

No matter what your methods, there is a good bid available.

West Deals + No One Vulnerable

	WEST	EAST	
	♠ K 9 8 7 6 3	♠ Q 10 4	
	♥ K 8	♥ A Q 5 2	
	♦ A Q 8	♦ 10 7 2	
	♣ 7 2	♣ J 8 4	

WEST	NORTH	EAST	SOUTH
1♠	Pass	2♠	Pass
Pass	Dbl	Rdbl	Pass
Pass	3♣	Pass	Pass
3♠	All pass		

THIS HAND SHOWS a theme that I don't see used at the table that much. West opens 1♠ and East correctly raises to 2♠.

North, in the balancing seat, comes back in with a takeout double. This does not promise much. Usually, a balancing bidder is counting on his partner to have some values.

East has a chance to contribute something here. Some players go straight to 3♠ with the East hand. Some players wait until South bids something and then they bid 3♠.

These players are all wrong. The correct bid with the East hand is redouble. This is not a great big noise. It doesn't say that East has discovered some extra points. It just says that East has a maximum hand for his bid. Since a raise to 2♠ can be made with as few as four high-card points plus some distribution, up to ten poor-quality points with balanced shape, there is a huge range of values for East to have.

A redouble says you have a nice eight or more. This bid helps West in three ways:

1. He may be able to compete to the three level.
2. He may be able to double the opponents.
3. He may choose to pass and stay uninvolved.

On the West hand above, West is pretty happy to bid 3♠. He might have done that anyway. But with East's redouble, he is extra pleased to do so.

Here are some additional examples of what West might bid:

♠ A 9 8 7 3
♥ 7 3
♦ A Q 7
♣ A 10 6

West might decide to double 3♣. I would be willing to take this chance. The odds are that your partner has three spades only and probably a balanced hand. If so, the opponents may be in trouble.

♠ A 9 8 7 3
♥ 7 3
♦ A 8
♣ Q J 10 7

This hand is barely worth an opening bid but it is definitely worth a double of 3♣. West has close to four tricks and East is showing nine or so points. It's a virtual certainty that 3♣ doubled is going down.

Note that East's redouble does not create a force. It just says that he has maximum points for his bidding. It is not reasonable that his redouble is forcing. If he has a good enough hand to go to 3♠, he should have made a limit raise or some equivalent on the first round.

Is East forbidden to bid 3♠ all by himself after North's balancing double? East may do so. However, if he does bid 3♠, he absolutely guarantees that he has four trumps. Four trumps doesn't make every hand worth a 3♠ bid but they are mandatory for hands where he does bid 3♠.

Here are two examples of this theme:

♠ Q 8 3
♥ Q 7 4 3
♦ Q 7 4
♣ Q 4 3

East should pass. East has only three trumps and his values are very poor.

♠ Q J 9 3
♥ 4 3
♦ Q J 4
♣ 9 8 7 3

This is a sane 3♠ bid over the double. East has four good spades, some shape, and a diamond holding that may prove useful. Note that bidding 3♠ immediately after the double has this advantage. It keeps South from bidding something.

West Deals   +   North-South Vulnerable

WEST	EAST
♠ 8 7 2	♠ Q J 9 6 5 4 3
♥ 4	♥ 10 7 6
♦ A K Q 10 6	♦ J 5
♣ A 8 7 4	♣ J

WEST	NORTH	EAST	SOUTH
1♦	1♥	3♠	4♥
4♠	All pass		

THERE'S AN OLD rule that says you shouldn't preempt opposite your partner's good hands. That is nonsense. East's jump to 3♠ shows a weak hand with a seven-card suit. That's exactly what East has. East knows he has a hand worth bidding with, but if he bids 1♠, West will expect more high cards. Note that if East-West were vulnerable, the suit would be slightly better. ♠AJ106543 would be about right.

Making a descriptive 3♠ bid informs West what's up and it really messes with the North-South bidding in the event they can make something. Preemptive bids are preemptive, but they are also descriptive.

POSTMORTEM

Note that a jump to 2♠ would be treated by many as a weak jump shift, most likely with six cards.

WEST

♠ 10 7
♥ A Q 6 5 3
♦ K Q 7
♣ Q 10 3

WEST	NORTH	EAST	SOUTH
1♥	1♠	4♥	4♠
?			

HERE IS AN everyday bidding problem. West's 1♥ meets with lots of competition. At the end, when South bids 4♠, what ought West to do?

Should he pass, double, or bid 5♥?

WEST	NORTH	EAST	SOUTH
1♥	1♠	4♥	4♠
All pass			

Here's the layout:

WEST		EAST	
♠ 10 7		♠ 6	
♥ A Q 6 5 3		♥ J 9 8 4 2	
♦ K Q 7		♦ 10 8	
♣ Q 10 3		♣ K 7 6 5 2	

West should pass. There are a number of reasons for this.

1. East's 4♥ bid is weak. I often see players jumping to 4♥ on this auction to tell partner they have points. I also see these players jumping to 4♥ when they have a preemptive hand. How in the world is opener supposed to know what to do?

   East, in situations like one, must make a value bid if he has a good hand and must reserve the jump to game to show weak hands.

2. Since East is weak, it is way against the odds that you can make 5♥. You rate to go down at least one trick and down three is possible if the opponents can get a couple of club ruffs.

   If East had a doubleton spade, 5♥ would go down even more.

3. Even if East has a weak hand, your side may have enough values to set 4♠. On the layout above, you could end up with a heart, two diamonds, and a club.

4. Remember this. South bid 4♠ over 4♥. He was under pressure and may have made a pushy bid. If you can set 4♠, it won't be good for you to go down a few in 5♥, doubled.

POSTMORTEM

The main theme of this hand is that East must show the kind of hand he has, and not raise to game with four points and with fourteen. Make bids your partner can understand.

North Deals + North-South Vulnerable

WEST	EAST
♠ 3 2	♠ A K J 10
♥ K 10 8 7 5 2	♥ 3
♦ J 4	♦ A 8 7 5
♣ A 8 2	♣ J 7 6 3

WEST	NORTH	EAST	SOUTH
	1♦	?	

You have a full opening bid. Is there a way into the bidding or should you pass?

WEST	NORTH	EAST	SOUTH
	1♦	1♠	Pass
2♥	Pass	?	

East has a hand that I would be in the bidding with, but many would not. The 1♠ overcall is fine with me. It meets the requirements for overcalling with a four-card suit.

1. Your hand is good, around opening bid strength.
2. Your four-card suit is very good.
3. You don't have the shape for a takeout double.
4. You can bid your suit at the one level.

Having bid 1♠, the bidding goes on. South passes and your partner bids 2♥, zeroing in on your singleton.

Firstly, are you allowed to pass?

If you decide you can pass, is that the best bid?

If you decide you want to bid again, what bid should you make?

WEST	NORTH	EAST	SOUTH
	1♦	1♠	Pass
2♥	All pass		

My agreements are that a new suit in response to an overcall is constructive but passable. This means that East can pass. Next is the question of whether you should pass. With a misfit and with no good source of tricks in sight, I suggest passing.

POSTMORTEM

Looking at both hands, you can see that notrump is not fetching. Certainly West has his 2♥ bid and certainly you can't make anything higher. The bigger issue here is that overcalling in a four-card suit can be good, but you need to know what the requirements are. If you don't have them, you should pass. One example only. RHO opens 1♦.

♠ 8 7 4
♥ A K Q 8
♦ 8 7 3
♣ 10 5 4

Pass. You have the good suit and you can bid at the one level but you don't have a good enough hand.